MW00616676

MOMENTS
to
MYSELF

MOMENTS
to
MYSELF

Living in the Now

KAMRI COLE

KP PUBLISHING COMPANY

ISBN: 978-1-950936-70-0 (Paperback)
ISBN: 978-1-950936-71-7 (Ebook)

Editor:	Melanie James
Cover Photo:	Lance Williams
Cover Design:	Christopher White
Interior Design:	James Sparkman
Literary Director:	Sandra Slayton James

Published by:
KP Publishing Company
Publisher of Fiction, Nonfiction & Children's Books
Valencia, CA 91355
www.kp-pub.com

Printed in the United States of America

To my younger self, I'm so proud of the woman you're blossoming into. This is the book that you needed to read coming into adulthood.

To the dreamers and those who feel lost, I wish to remind you of the light within you that still exists.

CONTENTS

ACKNOWLEDGMENTS

Thank you God for allowing me to experience your light and to become a vessel for your wisdom. Thank you for gifting me with creative energy and for giving me the will, obedience, and strength to do your work.

My sincere gratitude to my family and friends who have clung by my side during my personal journey. Your love and loyalty is held dear and fortifies me.

I also want to acknowledge the one who encouraged me to write this book, Laval Belle. Thank you for helping me see the light inside of me that I forgot existed. You have been a guardian angel, a friend, and a true gift to me.

INTRODUCTION

There's nothing that really prepares us for life—especially adulthood. We kind of just jump into the sea of life and struggle as we find our way. They say your 20s is when you find out who you really are. For me, I mastered to be who I was not. While I attended Howard University, I fell adrift amongst the crowd of my peers, but somehow always felt a lingering sense of loneliness.

Like most 20-year-olds, I struggled with post-grad depression while transitioning to the next phase of my life. I often found myself full of anxiety and paralyzed with fear of the unknown. I was learning to deal with the challenges of building new relationships, adjusting to new jobs, battling the fear of feeling left behind, all while trying to find deeper meaning within myself.

I've realized that as we grow older, we are confronted with new battles, life transitions, and more trial and error of figuring it all out. It's a never-ending cycle of trying to get the hang of things, but I discovered life doesn't have to be that complicated. There is a path you can walk down without constantly feeling entangled in the unknown of life. When you feel lost, you can easily gain clarity. I've come to understand that we already have access to all the answers; we just have to go within to receive them.

You may not realize it yet, but you are an extension of God. God is within you, and you have access to the power of all creation. Not everyone has this awareness; therefore, they do not understand how to tap in and utilize their power. This book is a beginner-friendly guide to learning to live a more spiritually-inclined life that you will use at different stages of your life to remind you of who you are. I will share with you how you can attract things into your life, experience a deeper relationship with yourself and God, and ultimately live in your divine potential.

Initially, I did not want to write this book. I was first told to write a book in November of 2017, and I said no because I thought I didn't have anything to say. Not to mention, I thought, who am I to write a self-help book when I still need to help myself? Well, destiny always outweighs desire, because, during the first seven months of 2018, God revealed everything I needed to say. Each month, I lived a different chapter of my book until I finally realized it was my duty to share this gift of knowledge I'd been given. I'd learned how to live in harmony with my true source, and it has completely changed my life forever. It's an unknown principle that I had been living by but never became aware of its power, and my ability to use it, until now.

The words in this book are only half mine because I truly believe I was just a vessel through which God's words needed to flow. Even as the author, I have been taken aback at the content presented in this book. Still, after reading my own work too many times to count, I am always reminded of something new or receiving exactly what I need to hear. Despite my astonishment, I've lived my book time and time again, and I want to extend my knowledge unto you so that you too may become conscious of your power to use it. That supernatural power is rooted in self-awareness and only extends deeper within your highest self. While we tear ourselves up worrying about our careers, relationships, and obtaining material things, we only keep ourselves further from what we really want and who we really are.

I would also like to add that I am in no way perfect

in implementing the ideas presented in this book. However, I am so much better because of it. This is the book I needed to read and will continue to read when I feel lost, overwhelmed, helpless, or confused while encountering life's many twists, turns, and transitions. It's the book I needed to remind me of who I really am so that I could boldly express all that I am.

This is not a self-help book made to exclusively inspire you to reach your earthly goals to acquire material things.

If that's what you're looking for, gift this book to someone else because it's not your time. It's a book designed to help you understand yourself better so that you may live up to your potential. I genuinely believe that this book will fall into the hands of each reader in divine time, so if you're still reading this, your time is now.

Welcome to learning to live in the moment. Join me on this journey and enjoy the beauty of life that miraculously unfolds.

I. AUTHENTICITY

UNDERSTANDING WHO YOU ARE

From birth we are taught how we ought to behave, what not to do, and how to be like everyone else in this world. At the same time, we're encouraged to be ourselves and be unique, which is contradictory to our society's framework. Living with this notion causes us to lose ourselves in other people's beliefs that often aren't true to us as individuals. When we can live beyond everyone's expectations, we begin to realize how ridiculous it is to follow this imaginary path of life and we will feel inspired to create our own. I can acknowledge that the unknown is a scary place, but it's almost like we operate under the fear of finding out who we really are and facing that reality. This change can be uncomfortable, but only because of the construct we've been conditioned to accept.

We may not realize it yet, but we are all creators.

We are all reflections of God's will because we have the power to manifest celestial gifts, speak life, and create. We create images, circumstances, and events that take place in our lives, whether we realize it or not. I'm sure you have heard of the law of attraction or the power of thought. Those are all philosophical words to describe accessing the power of God within you. The law of belief states that what you believe will eventually become true, and what is true to you shapes your reality. If we hold this much power, how can we not be extensions of God? We've been taught that we are separate from God and that power is above us, but it's actually within us.

At the very core of your being is a great "I am" statement. This statement enables you to strip away the ideas that society wants you to believe about who you are or who you should be. When you can get back to your intrinsic knowledge of self, you will begin to understand who you are on deeper levels. This journey is a part of the awakening process. It starts with the healing of your soul to awaken who you are and your connection to God. Once you have this understanding, you can never go back. Your spirit will thank you and rejoice, for it is more alive than ever. You are a limitless light being! Welcome, and enjoy the journey.

ACCEPTING WHO YOU ARE

When people say, "accept me as I am," some may interpret it as an excuse for being lazy, rude, unmotivated, or other undesirable traits. It can come off as passive, but that may not always be the case. Self-acceptance, requires acknowledgement and an honest assessment of who you are in every moment of life. We must admit that we are who we are, but it doesn't mean that we will be that way forever. For example, it doesn't mean if you rob a bank and get caught, you say, "well, that's me, I'm a bank robber, and I won't change. It is what it is." It means that our characteristics, responses, and judgments make up how we operate in the world in our unique way, and all of these things are subject to change for the better.

Everyone has a right to their individuality and should be encouraged to embrace it. Often, without realizing it, we yield to the crowd and negate the traits that make us unique. First, because we don't understand who we are, but fundamentally because we aren't willing to accept all that we are. In doing so, we can become beings with suppressed trauma. Trauma that cuts so deep it leaves scars that can last for years and even decades. When learning to accept ourselves, we must address all factors, even the truths that hurt us most. One of the first steps to fully owning who you are is accepting all that you are. Understanding yourself on this level will require you to be honest about how you feel towards all things in your life. Instead of looking at things as how your emotions color them, you will have to go deep inside yourself to find what's real.

Discovering ourselves requires us to take our masks off and reveal our true selves. Not just to ourselves but to the world. This is easier said than done, especially when you've lived the majority of your life hiding behind a mask and having become comfortable wearing it. I'm definitely guilty of putting up the front of "having-it-all-together" when underneath everything was falling apart. After I graduated from University, from June to December, I practically lived and breathed wearing that mask. If you asked me how my life was going, I would say it was great! That was about 60% fabrication, and 40% hope. The good thing about wearing a mask is it can sometimes protect you from hurting, but only temporarily. The bad thing is that you end up hiding who you really are and prevent yourself from connecting with others in a substantive way. One can only wear a mask for so long before it becomes uncomfortable, and you want to take it off and be yourself.

At some point in our lives, we all struggle with self-acceptance. With society constantly shoving unrealistic expectations in our face, it's hard to appreciate ourselves for who we truly are. We hide our flaws, we stay secretive about our pasts, and even shun others for embodying traits in ourselves that we don't like or don't have. What is it about ourselves that we aren't willing to accept?

- We don't want to accept that we are not "where we want to be" in life because we haven't put in the real work.
- We don't want to accept the fact that we can be selfish or wrong.
- We don't want to accept that we've caused hurt in other people's lives.
- We don't want to accept the hurt in our own lives.
- We don't want to accept the fact that our partner may be happier with someone else.

The bottom line is we don't want to accept the things that hurt our ego.

Some of us, on the other hand, feel like we have accepted our true selves. We've read all the self-help books, changed our diet, started working out, started making more money, and have more friends. Compared to others, it feels like you're actually doing better in life. You may have nicer things, have more followers on social media, and you may get to take lavish vacations throughout the year. You may have even labeled yourself as the one who "has it all together," or the "go-getter" of your friend group. You've embraced this role that you assumed, and you like it. You embrace it because it makes you feel good, primarily because other people like it. With this, I have to ask you, do you accept you, or do you accept your ego?

Sometimes we find it hard to accept all parts of ourselves when other people can't seem to validate us. We live in fear of exposing the parts of us that aren't the norm because our ego won't let us be judged or criticized. Ego then tries to protect us by keeping the vulnerable side of us hidden from the world, and sometimes hidden from ourselves. Only when we are stronger than our ego, can we choose to love and accept all of the things that make us unique. For those of you thinking, "but what about when we are confident in who we are, and other people still don't want to accept us?" Let it be. When you have accepted all that you are, you don't need anyone's approval over how you live your life. You must simply just be. Yet, our greatest desire in life is to feel accepted, understood and loved for who we really are. So yes, it is frustrating when people can't seem to give us that. We are quick to blow them off as haters, but I do have to ask, do you want them to accept you or accept your ego?

The truth is, most of us walk around with two versions of ourselves. One, is our true self, which is impeccable, loving, and undisturbed by trauma, criticism, or a need to conform to the box society has created. The other is the version of ourselves we've let the world mold to fit prescribed norms, otherwise known as the ego. The ego's primary role is to separate you from the truth of who you are—a light being who is already complete; mentally and spiritually healthy. It's like a machine that requires constant lubrication with pride, praise, possessions, and power. The ego believes the road to happiness includes material success, achievement, fame, and acceptance from others. But your unconditioned self, the real you, the God in you, is so much more than that. It already knows how to fulfill you and make you whole.

The happiness you have been looking for outside of you can finally be yours when you stop chasing and start choosing. The more we are willing to accept and love ourselves, the less we desire to go looking for it in all the wrong places. This is usually how we find ourselves staying in jobs we hate or spending money we don't have. When we are comforted by our self-love, we no longer need to find comfort through external vices.

Start loving yourself by exercising forgiveness. Forgive yourself for:

- All the times you have allowed your ego to block your joy.
- Putting the weight of society's expectations on your shoulders.
- Ever thinking you are less than the powerful beam of light that you are.

Understand that the primary reason you need to forgive is to restore yourself to the authentically happy person you are here to be.

There is resistance to self-acceptance by people who think having control is essential for their psychological survival. The need for control is not necessarily bad; however, it serves as an expression of your lower self, fueled by both fear and desire. The more secure you are in yourself, the less external validation you need. You don't need to one-up people, seek approval, or prove your worth to anyone. Think about how much emotional energy you put towards maintaining appearances, or doing everything to prevent yourself from being negatively judged. Congratulations, you have mastered being who you are not!

Now I want you to imagine a lamp as three layers of self: a light bulb, which is covered in dirt, and on top of that, a lamp shade. The light bulb represents the most authentic version of ourselves—who we really are. The dirt represents all of our insecurities, self-doubt, and flaws—who we fear we are. The lamp shade represents the self that we pretend to be—who we project we are. For most of us, our sense of self-worth is false. We live our lives seeing ourselves as the lamp shade instead of the light inside. It's because we fear that other people will see our dirt, so we mask ourselves with a cover to "be okay." Similar to the lighting inside of a house, you must clean your light-bulbs to brighten your home; otherwise, you'll find yourself wasting energy. Instead of doing the work to clean the dirt off your light, most people choose to *cover* their dirt with job titles, material possessions, social media pages, religion, or even a relationship status. While that is a temporary way to soothe your pain, there's a more fruitful and joyous way that is both effortless and powerful. It's starting from the inside out, simply accepting who you are—a beautiful beam of light.

Acceptance isn't about liking or approving something. It is about letting life unfold and flow without getting in the way. For many of us, our first impulse is to resist something that we do not like that comes our way. Acceptance requires overriding this impulse, choosing to breathe into and through the experience, trusting that it has value and is for us, not against us. The truth of the matter is that resistance prolongs our negative experience, and acceptance welcomes the possibility of changing our experiences by changing our attitude.

It's difficult to understand the paradox between accepting something negative about yourself and striving for positive change. The main thing holding you up is your mind saying, "I don't want it to be like this." When you resist the reality of the situation, you hand over the power of your emotional well-being to other people's reality. You become easily triggered or start living by how other people perceive you to fill the void. This is only feeding and hurting your ego all at the same time. Ask yourself, do you need to act in a certain way according to your expectations and desires for you to be happy? Can you let go of this idea of who you should be in this exact moment of your life and start accepting who you are?

We judge ourselves for not being where we think we should be in life or for simply making a mistake. We forget that our worth doesn't come from our career accomplishments, bank account, or material possessions, and we're left empty when we try to find it within those attainments. Think about how we treat children and babies. A child isn't going to earn a lot of money, win awards, or try to do anything to prove their worth. A child isn't even concerned with such earthly matters until we program their minds to the standards we were programmed to live by. They make mistakes daily, but we love and accept them anyway as they are. At what age does that not become acceptable anymore? We should continue giving ourselves and others this unconditional love and the right to live in a judge-free zone.

I had the hardest time getting a job after graduating college. For two months during the summer, I spent almost every day applying for jobs in Los Angeles. I received no responses. This was extremely disappointing and frightening to me because I worked consistently throughout college. Getting jobs and internships came so easy to me, so I was confused as to why this post-grad life was the complete opposite. At this point, I was extremely stressed. I saw all my peers going on vacation for graduation, moving into their new apartments, and starting their first day at their corporate jobs. Meanwhile, I was at home struggling to keep myself from sinking into post-grad depression.

Eventually, I stopped judging my situation and learned to find the good in it. I accepted my situation, not in the sense that I compromised my worth, or became complacent in life; I said yes to allowing God to move through me and got out of the way of what God was trying to do. We're all living in disappointment and suffering when we're guided by our ego's expectations. However, if we can quiet down our ego, we can hear God ordering our steps to lead us on our divine path.

Let's begin to become comfortable exploring our unique truths along our journey. Let's be more open and honest about all things that we consider to be our wins and losses. It is a disservice to ourselves and the rest of the world when we are not embracing all that we are, flaws included. What we fail to realize is that those flaws connect us on a deep and emotional level. If it's genuine, that level of vulnerability is usually protected with love and lives in a safe space. I challenge you to be brave enough to live in that space, even when it doesn't seem so safe. I know it's hard, though, because our ego is always trying to protect us from what it thinks will hurt us. It gets in the way of allowing us to experience this kind of emotional breakthrough because we fear we'll be judged, rejected, used, or misunderstood. Nothing real can be misunderstood, and a wise woman once said, nothing real can be broken.

When we can accept who we are, the "good" and the "bad," we can be more accepting of others. Most of the time, when there is something about someone else we don't accept, it is because we don't accept it within ourselves. More often than not, we judge others based on our personal opinions, which only shuts the door on experiencing any real connection. However, when we can accept ourselves for who we are, we accept others as they are, rather than who we want them to be. This opens the door welcoming the greatest power of all—*Love*.

EMBRACING WHO YOU ARE

By choosing to love yourself, you can begin to embrace who you are, for all that you are. First, we have to understand that we are all worthy and created with love. In choosing to share our love with other people and things, we can forget to direct it back to ourselves. It's easy to recognize other people as being worthy of love because of our distorted perception of what their life is and what love is. We equate the worthiness of love with success, fame, money, race, or sexuality. By doing so, we exclude others from experiencing love. Love is not exclusive. Hate is. And sometimes we can love everyone, except ourselves.

Self-hate is more common than most people would believe. It is usually developed over time and can have several causes. Some of us put unreasonable expectations on ourselves that often lead to us falling short and feeling like we have failed. Our inner critic shows up and makes us feel ashamed by telling us how disappointing we've been. However, more often than that, our self-hate derives from false expectations from others. By trying to connect with other people, we think that we have to do so by meeting their expectations because when they are satisfied with us, we are satisfied with ourselves. Nonetheless, when we aren't able to meet the expectations of other people, we begin to feel devalued because we disappointed them. Once again, our inner critic comes creeping in and says that we have failed this person and are not worthy of being valued or loved by them.

Our self-hate can also derive from traumatic

experiences that have been mentally and emotionally disturbing. These experiences can be sexual, emotional, physical, mental or neglectful. As a result of our trauma from abuse, we then view the world through lenses tainted by these experiences. In an attempt to make the most of what we know our life to be, our inner critic tells us that we are not valuable or worthy. This could be something someone once told us, or how a specific situation made us feel. When we think to ourselves, "Do I want or need to experience this?" what we're really saying is, "Do I deserve to experience this?" What our inner critic will say is "no"—denying ourselves what we desire. However, by rejecting ourselves, we feel like we are winning by beating other people to it. We reject ourselves first before anyone else can.

This form of self-rejection is not always as pronounced as depression, suicidal thoughts, self-harm, or other destructive behaviors. It can present itself in the jobs you apply for, the clothes you wear, the women or men you approach, or even how you wear your hair. We deny ourselves because we fear how other people will respond to us. We fear not meeting their expectations, disappointing them, or being rejected. When we have the desire to approach people that we find appealing, our inner critic tells us, "they are too good for us, you are not worthy." Under these circumstances we often avoid building connections with people because the rejection feels a lot more comfortable coming from ourselves than from others.

Another way we sabotage our progress is in our careers. If there is a career we've dreamed of exploring, we'll tell ourselves, "I can't do that." We then seek positions far from our dreams or perhaps in jobs in the same industry. Aspiring sports players will become sports agents or sports hosts. Aspiring singers or musicians will try to find fulfillment in becoming an artist manager or an artist and repertoire (A&R) scout. While there are people who dream of having these careers, some of us will hide behind these positions, limiting ourselves from achieving our dreams, but still try to get as close as possible to the lifestyle. Some of us can admit that at one point, we've rejected the idea of believing we are worthy of our dreams. Ultimately, when we deny ourselves of our most authentic and deep desires, we deny God's divine plan for our lives.

While I was in University, I felt like I couldn't be open about my interest in acting because I hadn't revealed that side of myself to anyone. I was suppressing part of myself instead of embracing my truth. I realized that I never needed a grand announcement, approval, or permission from anyone to be who I already was, but sadly many of us feel like we do. We grow up feeling like we have to be accepted, just to survive. In those times, we ask ourselves, "who am I?" but what we're really asking is, "who do I need to be, to be loved?" We then try to squeeze our entire being into one persona, and while doing that, we suppress all the parts of ourselves that don't fit in this constructed image.

We live in a society considered oppressive by many, so we often feel like we have to choose our battles in the face of that oppression. We can't choose our race, but we can choose our religion. These decisions are rooted in our desire to be loved and connected with others. It's more comfortable to show parts of ourselves that are widely accepted by society because we fear the authentic version of ourselves will be rejected. You have to stop chasing others and start choosing you. I've grown to learn that people don't care as much as you think they do. As often as we judge ourselves, it's hard to imagine that someone wouldn't judge us for showing an unfamiliar side. The truth is most people are attracted to and interested in people that are unapologetically themselves. Our authenticity—stripped of a facade—is illuminating and refreshing. We think we are making other people feel uncomfortable by embracing who we are, when in reality, we are just hurting ourselves when we don't. We can't expect to live our entire lives based on the comfort of others, so why not embrace the things that make you unique, even if it makes others uncomfortable.

If we want to experience the power that is already within us, we have to be willing to express our most genuine and authentic selves. Often we are the ones getting in our way. We choose not to see ourselves as great and powerful beings because we don't have the money or fame to prove it. I want you to look at yourself as someone who has the power to be your own hero, but first, you have to love and embrace your power to use it.

II. FOLLOW YOUR OWN PATH

WHO ARE YOU?

No one knows you like you know yourself. Considering that God lives within, your intuition always knows what's best for you and your divine path. Our deepest desire is to satisfy the part of us that wants to walk on that path. Initiating that journey begins when we have clarity on who we are, what we are, and where we are.

From early childhood, we're asked, "what do you want to be when you grow up?" We can feel the pressure to give an answer that will impress. As we grow older, we begin to learn more about ourselves and develop a greater understanding of our desires and talents. Granted, our desires are often fueled and colored by society, but they are our own, and they help us decide how we want to live our life.

Often, we think our careers should prove to the world who we are. We can get so caught up in what we believe a job can do for us, rather than choosing to take on the real job inside of us without the job title. In other words, we want career paths that look appealing, so we can prove ourselves as valuable. Everyone will tell you to follow your own path, and you'll find success. Do we know what that truly means? While it's great to have the opportunity to walk along paths that others have paved for us, you'll find much more fulfillment by walking along your unique path. This requires us to have a greater awareness and deeper understanding of ourselves.

Most of our life experiences are a result of our mental and emotional responses—our thoughts and our words. It is our programming, distorted beliefs, and fears that impact our ability to put our heart-centered selves "out there" to be seen by others. As you begin to peel away all the barriers around YOU, you will start to see that you are so much more than you have decided you are.

At the end of the day, none of this job stuff really matters in the grand scheme of things. Work can be a deep source of meaning in our lives, but it should never come at the expense of our ability to be present for life. Our jobs do not define who we are or the value we have to offer. Our parents and teachers aren't necessarily the ones to blame, but they constantly shove the ideas of who they think we should "be" when we grow older. Character traits, like "being a nice human, having a kind heart and loving others" are often secondary. So in this society, we think we have to "be" our jobs because our job serves as a representation of who we are. You are not your job. Despite the power, money, or responsibilities, your job title does not define all that you are. If it did, you wouldn't need a title; you'd just be you. The truth of the matter is that your job is just what you do on the way to becoming all that you are, and who you're becoming is entirely up to you.

I started living my dreams when I quit my survival job. Before then, I never truly understood what it meant to be living life rather than making a living. While I was working, going door-to-door to sell phone service, I thought I was my job. An annoying, desperate salesperson. I was embarrassed to tell people what I did, so I painted it up with words like, "I do marketing and sales." Who did I think I was fooling? Myself, clearly. I wanted to change who I thought I was on the inside, so I could change how I thought others would see me on the outside. I didn't realize that I was the same person who is now living my life, waking up every day grateful for another chance to be myself, while doing the things I love.

Regardless of what it is that I do for money, I am much more than that. I know I'm a person of love. My energy is powerful, and I want others to feel love when they have an encounter with me. This is wherever I work. Whether I have the highest paying job or the lowest of job responsibilities, I am grateful for life, the opportunity to have employment, and for everything that is to come.

It took my arrival in a better place for my ego to finally allow me to express the truth about my life. I am no longer hiding my truth, and I don't have to justify myself to anyone. I wish I'd learned this sooner. I wish that more of us could release our ego enough to live in our truth. It starts with accepting who we really are. Not our job titles, not our classification, not our race, and not our bank account. We are all supernatural beings of light having a human experience to serve as an expression of God here on Earth. How each of us goes about doing that is what makes our divine paths so unique.

WHAT DO YOU WANT TO DO?

Ask yourself these questions:

- Why are you in the career field that you're in?
- What are you looking to gain out of your career experience?
- Why do you want to be where you want to be?
- Do you want to have a lot of money so you can feel at peace?
- Do you want to have power so you can feel respected?
- Do you want to have fame so you can feel validated?

Do you believe that achieving and acquiring external things will provide you the ultimate fulfillment? Everything that you are seeking to have is not external; it's all internal. It's already inside of you. You just have to become attuned to your inner-self to realize it. Everyone possesses divine power, but it is our responsibility to cultivate that power and direct it to emulate love. We are all on the path to realizing that we are masters of our reality. We will remain in a state of suffering until we decide to see the light inside of us and become aware of the thoughts and practices that help us shine.

The reason we all have triggers that spark our light

is so we can use this force within us to manifest, create, and push forward in our unique way. Passion serves as a driving force for breaking boundaries (some of which are self-imposed) and accomplishing our goals. What separates you from that which you don't like to do and what you do like to do is passion.

When we create things we're passionate about, we allow ourselves to be a vessel for God's divine expression. For the evolution of this world, we must find it as our duty to share our gifts and openly present our unique selves to the world. When we do this, we spark inspiration in others and ultimately create a snowball effect of joy and love. Instead of chasing material things, shift your focus to what's going to keep you going through the times when you want to give up. No matter what you're doing, you will experience those moments. It's more fulfilling undergoing temporary trials with something that feeds you emotionally, spiritually, and mentally, versus pursuing something that only feeds your bank account.

When you have passion, you're inclined to see the bigger picture. Whether it is a business, hobby, or political/social movement, if it's an endeavor you're passionate about, it will hold more importance to you. As a result, you will be more dedicated to building that business, mastering that craft, or standing firm in making change for your beliefs. Choosing to let go of chasing a paycheck and deciding to follow your dreams, will ultimately lead you to a road of satisfaction. If it's something you're truly passionate about and believe is the path you must travel, you will inevitably encounter satisfaction as long as you don't give up.

When you believe in something and proceed to manifest that idea into physical form, you build confidence in yourself. Receiving physical manifestations or recognition helps validate what we already know on the inside to be true. This encourages us to have more faith in our intuitive nature and gives us the determination to achieve whatever it is that we believe. It also serves as a natural fuel that sparks action. You can have relentless energy, but without passion, you cannot withstand the persistent challenges.

Passionate people are focused because they have clarity about what they want to achieve in life. Many people are passionate about various pursuits, but they don't have the clarity on what they should do with their passions. You may be one of those people asking yourself, "What do I do? How do I make this work?" Well, for starters, you must have an awareness of who you are.

It's easy to get caught up in seeing ourselves through other people's eyes. We then fall victim to making decisions based on how other people will perceive us. The solution to that is taking a step back and seeking clarity on who you are, what you value, and what you ultimately want. Most people aren't born passionate about a certain endeavor; but once discovered, they build on it. To find your passion, you have to be open to trying new ventures and exploring different spaces. If you feel like you haven't found your path you're passionate to walk on, it may be attributable to any of these three reasons.

1. You know what you want to do, but you're too afraid to do it.

2. You're too comfortable living beneath your potential.

3. You're too busy trying to survive, that you can't thrive.

All of these reasons are products of fear. The first one is quite normal. If you fall underneath this truth, then start small. Begin incorporating what-ever you're passionate about in your everyday life in small ways. If you like to paint, begin painting in your spare time. Then if you choose to do so, find a way to monetize this hobby. Start small and slowly work your way to building a lifestyle out of doing what brings you fulfillment. If doing what you want to do requires you to move across the country, MAKE THAT MOVE! I know things are easier said than done, however, things undone can never be done, so get to doing!

The second one is more interesting to me because it's more common than most people think. It's this strange and honest idea that we find ourselves being too afraid to live to our fullest potential. We want success, but in all honesty, some of us are too afraid to actually do what it takes to get there. Some of us are worried about who we will have to become to reach what we want, and some of us are afraid of what we'll have to do to get there.

The third reason describes the person who is stuck in fight mode and can't live in flight. This looks like you finding comfort in your survival job or not being able to grow out of a survival mindset. Every decision you make is based on your need to survive, whether that's with stability or worthiness. You're so busy trying to live a picture-perfect life that you don't give yourself time to focus on the things that actually ignite your spirit. Again, give yourself a taste of what it feels like to immerse yourself in the things that bring you joy. Trust yourself.

Being held back by any of these thoughts is equally damaging, so you must push through your fears to live the life you deserve. I intentionally state that you should push through rather than get rid of it because fear itself isn't all bad. When you allow fear to prevent you from moving forward in life, that's when you're succumbing to the illusion of fear.

Now, if you truly have not the slightest idea of what you're passionate about, here is a list of questions you can ask yourself:

1. What makes my heart full?
2. If I weren't getting paid, what would I spend the rest of my life doing?
3. What allows me to be creative?
4. What am I naturally good at?
5. What is one thing that I can't live without doing?
6. What is something I can do that will bring me peace?
7. What kind of life do I want to live?
8. How do I define success?

Take a moment to answer these questions, and open yourself up to receiving the answers that are already within you. When you find your clarity, the next step for you is to take action.

Some people don't have the clarity to know what it is they want to be doing in life or even the next steps they should take. One thing they can agree on is that they want to make a difference in the world or just live a better life for themselves. I'm sure that's something a lot of us desire, and to those of you who don't know where to start or what that looks like, here's the key: *love and happiness*.

The best thing you or anyone can do for this world is to be of love. To be of love, you must be filled with love. To be filled with love, you must be open to love. To be open to love, you must be connected to God. When you're connected to God, you find yourself always creating, whether it's a project, business, or romance. This requires us to dig deep inside of ourselves to know what really brings us joy. All of us came here to express our divinity in some shape or form and we are here to create, love and enjoy. Don't allow society to bark at you with what they think you should be "doing" to bring you fulfillment. Only you know what truly makes your heart full, and we should all be doing whatever feels right for our soul.

But above all, keep this in mind. God doesn't care what we "do". We didn't come here to do any specific job at all. We came here so that divinity could experience itself through this body. The real journey we walk on has nothing to do with anything external because every step is really an internal journey. It's not about time and accomplishing goals by a certain age; it's about being present and being able to live fully in every single moment. The question of "What do I *do* in life," is completely valid and should be given much consideration. However, the better question is, "How do I live in harmony with my soul, my true nature?"

WHERE YOU ARE VS. WHERE YOU WANT TO BE

Some people know what to do to make their passions their main focus in life, but it's no surprise that the excuses as to why they aren't doing it are plentiful. I hear, "I can't get up and move across the country," "I know, but what if it doesn't work out," "I want to get a stable job first," "I need to be secure first," or "I don't have enough money." All of these statements are completely understandable as to why someone wouldn't be able to move forward in living their dreams. Still, there's a difference between identifying an obstacle that you plan to get over and affirming an obstacle that you plan to use as validation for why you haven't gotten yourself together.

We can't continue to blame other people or circumstances when our situation doesn't fit the picture of the life we thought we would live. It's unfair to those people, and most importantly, it's unfair to yourself. We must take responsibility for our multiple singular actions that have led us to the condition of our lives in this present moment. The good news is that if you don't like the way your life looks right now, you have the power to change. Just recognize that changing your life externally requires that you first change internally.

If you can accept that you have power over your life, you can begin to bear witness to all of the manifestations you bring into your physical world through your subconscious mind. Your spirit wants to experience the joy of thriving and is waiting for you to give birth to your gifts. So what are you going to do to fulfill this burning desire? If you continue to compromise your true nature by seeking love and approval from others, then you're going to walk on a path that will bring out your demons, where you will ultimately be forced to face your fears.

We are so accustomed to living in a comfort zone that being imprisoned in the "reality of society" feels much safer. Fear, routine, procrastination, comparing yourself to others, and self-doubt are all the things that are keeping us trapped from experiencing the magic of what we can do. The sky is not the limit; you are. Your life is boundless, and so are your possibilities. If you want to live the life you've always dreamed of, you must first conquer your mind and push through fear.

We all have a vision of how we want our lives to look. Most of us desire to live comfortable, stress-free, and happy lives. We tend to set goals thinking that we have to accomplish them before we can live the life we want. What's holding us back from reaching those goals is ourselves. We are all trying to survive by seeking love and approval from others, so we try to find positions that will deem us worthy to receive it from everyone in the world. Is that the key to happiness? Money? Well, a lot of people make it seem that securing the bag and minding your business is the ultimate goal in life. This couldn't be further from the truth of what everyone's actually seeking—love. We all just want love. That's what our source energy knows, and that's what we need to survive. The way we go about obtaining that love can either be harmful or helpful.

We spend most of our lives working at a job, and a good portion of us aren't fulfilled at our jobs. Why is this? First, there are obvious reasons, such as institutional and structural racism, sexism, and other biases but aside from those, it's because most of us are chasing a paycheck instead of chasing our hearts. Think about how much happier the world would be if we were all doing what we loved? Yet, here we are, getting caught up in the matrix, working our survival jobs unfulfilled and unsatisfied.

I say we should all look for joy, not a job. If we can find ourselves working on whatever it is that fills us with joy and love, we can collectively spread that joy and feed each other with love, the way we're supposed to. The problem is, most of the time, the path to working this joyful job, doesn't always start out that way. Most career paths don't look anything like what we imagined ourselves doing in the beginning. Therefore, we don't stick with it through the end. It almost looks like achieving what we ultimately want is impossible, but it's the steps that we MUST take.

You always know you're on the right path when things miraculously fall into place. A year ago, when I quit my job, I had no idea how I was going to pay my rent, eat, or really do anything. When I first moved to Los Angeles and began working in sales, God told me that I would only be working there until December. December came, and I found myself still working there.

We had to complete a Personal Development Project, which descriptively detailed our values, goals, and life-long achievements. If we hadn't turned it in by January 1, we would be fired. So here I was on December 30, madly typing what would eventually become a 7-page essay on what I imagined my life to look like and the steps I would take to get there. After completing this assignment, I realized that I was nowhere near on-track to do any of the things I had planned and hoped for. I was instead using all of my time trying to make money just to barely get by. I knew that I wasn't supposed to be working there past December, but if I wasn't working there, where would I work?

There was so much internal conflict happening within me. I knew I didn't like my job and wasn't supposed to work there any longer, but I didn't know what my life would look like if I quit. So I fasted for 30 days to gain clarity on what my next move would be. The last week of my fast was also the last week of working at my job. I still hadn't figured out all the kinks of what I would do to support myself, but I knew continuing to direct all my time and energy towards something that wasn't helping me get closer to fulfillment was only going to hinder me rather than help me.

The following Monday, my first day of unemployment could not have felt more liberating. I was happier in my life than I had ever been before. I woke up with gratitude pouring out of my heart, and surely enough, I was receiving everything I needed and asked for. I had found a way to sustain and actually improve my lifestyle. God fulfilled all my requests and completely erased all worry from my heart. This was my testimony for when I began living a life rather than making a living. I've seen the same order of events happen for my friends when they too decided they would step out from their comfortable paychecks and choose to live their dreams. Everything just ends up working out and coming together, but only when you decide to take that first step on your divine path.

EMOTIONAL GUIDANCE

One of the problems that arise when we start walking on our divine path is that we encounter situations that don't look like how we think they should, so we reject them. Rather than being open to all possibilities, we try to calculate how everything should go or how our lives should look. When our next blessing comes into our lives, we may not even recognize it, and we may reject it before even exploring that path. When we do find the courage to explore those paths, we judge them harshly. We can feel like we've taken a step backward in life. It is not what happens that holds you back, but your judgmental beliefs about the situation or circumstance. Our perception of our current situation indicates whether we are allowing things to flow into our lives or not.

Esther and Jerry Hicks, the authors of *Ask and It Is Given*, introduced me to the idea of the emotional guidance system. The authors state that the emotional guidance system serves as our personal navigation to guide us to manifest the desires we do and do not want. When you are feeling negative emotions—fear, jealousy, anger, shame, or doubt—you are out of alignment with who you really are. When you are feeling positive emotions—love, happiness, appreciation, and gratitude—you are in alignment with who you really are. We are all energetic beings, and the laws of the Universe are always responding to the vibrations we send out. Most people only respond to what they are observing in their experience instead of being proactive and offering up a higher vibration, which then invites more of those positive feelings and experiences.

A lot of us wake up each morning and sigh and groan about all the things we have to do that day, or just by the simple thought that we have to go to work. Some of us spend our mornings feeling dreadful because of this. By emitting these negative thoughts in the morning, we attract negative experiences throughout the rest of our day and get stuck in a cycle of experiencing a life that is unfulfilled and lacking joy.

After realizing this, I decided to wake up every morning with gratitude. I may write down a list of all the things that I'm grateful for, some of which include my family, friends, love, new opportunities, grace, having a job, or my apartment being clean. The list can go on and on. Afterward, I'll meditate, read a book, or write out my feelings. By doing all these things that give me joy, I am aligning myself to send out positive vibrations that align with who I really am—a powerful light being.

Other people set their intentions with how they want their day to go by writing all the things they want to happen that day. Either way, it's important that regardless of how mundane our lives seem to be or how busy we get, we make time to take a moment to slow down, appreciate the fact that we have another day of life, and live in the moment. Ask yourself, what are some things you can do to bring higher vibrations to your morning?

Doing this doesn't mean that we have to spend our entire lives monitoring our thoughts or trying to block ourselves from experiencing negative thoughts. It simply means that we just need to always be aware of our feelings. Also, be aware that our emotional guidance system is just one sector of how we have the power to manifest things into our lives. It is not the end all be all, however it is a great foundation towards taking control over what you attract into your life.

When you ask for something, your request will always be granted in some form. The problem is we are not always positioning ourselves to receive what we're asking for. So with those of us who have decided to walk on our divine path, we find ourselves frustrated when the things we desire haven't manifested into physical form. The key is to be in alignment with the energy of our desire by putting out positive vibrations, a.k.a. "good vibes."

An example is, let's say I'm working at a job I don't like, and I want a better one. If I'm constantly focusing on how much my co-workers annoy me, how little I get paid, or how unprofessional my boss is,

I'm keeping my focus towards all the things that I don't want, thus preventing me from aligning myself to receiving what I do want—a new job. If I shift my focus and begin to imagine myself working at another job and think about how happy I will be working there and visualize my new lifestyle with my new paycheck, I am aligning myself with the energy of my desire to receive a new job. Once we become aware of our vibrational energy, we can be more proactive in creating the lives we strongly desire.

TAKE A RISK AND DON'T LOOK BACK

Once you've decided to walk on your divine path, there is no going back. Keep in mind this path is not career-based. It's walking down a path of self-discovery, reminding you that you are a co-creator of your world because God is within you. Our creations always start internally and manifest externally, so this journey will take you deeper within yourself and to higher places in the physical world. You just have to keep going, no matter what, and be open to receiving ALL that is in store for you, regardless of how your ego judges it.

I don't consider taking the first step in following your dreams as a risk because it's not. What's the risk if this is what was intended for you? I think it's more of a gamble to not follow and live your dreams because that's not the divine plan. You'll end up in a constant battle with yourself, which will manifest in physical form. It'll almost seem like things just can't go right.

Evaluate your life and see if you are walking on your divine path or the path that society has tried to herd you into. When you find yourself moving in alignment with what's for you, you have to keep going because breathtaking moments and pure love is waiting to be explored. Walking on this path isn't always easy. However, God is always with us, talking to and guiding us. We just have to be tuned-in to listen.

III. IN TUNE

DIVINE CONNECTION

When you are in tune with your body, your self-awareness is in harmony with your energy. You are more mindful of what is being communicated to you because you are the receiver through which the voice of God speaks. This is the state people are in when they hear God talking to them.

Tuning yourself to match the frequency of your highest self to receive messages is the same thing as tuning the radio to your favorite station to hear music or news being broadcasted. When the radio is not in tune, we hear that annoying, loud, staticky *shhhcchchkkkhshshzzfz* sound, or another station (that we don't even want) playing in the far background. We keep turning the dial until we finally get our radio to reach the station that we want to hear. Just as we have to tune our radio to our favorite station, we have to tune ourselves to receive the words of God. If not, we hear white noise—the loud and misguided opinions of society, and we find ourselves getting caught up in trying to absorb ideas that don't match our frequency.

When we are connected with our inner selves, we can function at our highest potential. We can go with the flow and accept growth and change as a natural part of life. When we can align with God, we can tune in to others. This moves us toward a state of love and understanding for one another. Rather than trying to control other people for how we would like for them to be or behave, we can accept them for who they are and appreciate them as their own divine being.

It is essential to align ourselves with our true nature so that we can be easily guided along our divine path. How we go about doing that is utilizing our intuition. It is what we describe as the voice that talks to us, offering clarity when we are confused and looking for answers. It gives us signs as to what paths we need to take, what doors we need to walk through, which people we need to speak with, and everything we need to be fulfilled.

Everyone has their own journey to navigate and while there are many principles that can be universal, no one else knows what's best for you more than you. Rather than focusing on the loud voices of the world, it's necessary to have the ability to tune in to yourself to receive guidance while navigating your path. Just know that, even though you may not be able to always hear God, God always hears you. God lives in you, so no matter how far away you think you are, God remains there underneath your built-up logic waiting for you to open the door to your heart.

There are many ways we can tune ourselves into ourselves and strengthen our intuition. First, you have to make a conscious decision that you are going to shift your focus from the ways of the world to the ways of your highest self. This may seem like a minuscule task, but you'd be surprised how much one small shift of focus can impact your life. Next, you want to find out what clears your mind and brings you peace. I will share with you the actions I take to keep myself tuned in, and I encourage you to practice one or all of them.

WRITING

For me, writing has always been a way to clear my mind and give me peace. I started writing in journals in the first grade. This was a way to express my most intimate, raw, and sometimes painful thoughts.

I never allowed anyone to read my journals, so I never held anything back. I would write the vilest thoughts and scribble myself out of the feeling of anger. I wouldn't stop writing until I felt peace.

This was my form of therapy—talking to myself to relieve myself of any negative emotions I would feel. However, I didn't always write when I felt upset or angry. There would be times where I would pray to God in the form of writing, or thank God for life, or just outline my day. What I didn't realize was that as I was expressing deep thoughts of mine that were true for me and from the heart, I was building a deeper connection to my inner self. I was in-tune with the very thoughts that were racing through my mind, and I used writing as a way to spell them out. If anyone asked me how I felt about something, I already knew because I had taken the time to write myself out of my feelings to get to the very core of what it is that I genuinely felt.

Sometimes we can get so entangled in how our feelings move us that we can't speak on what our heart truly feels. Our feelings are valid, but they are not always true. For example, let's say you're upset with your significant other because they're spending more time working than giving you attention. You may either express that you are displeased with them for working at their job so much, you want to leave them because you don't feel appreciated, or you may even act on your feelings and cheat. You may feel justified in doing any of these things, because of what your feelings "tell" you. However, if you can tune-in to what your heart is actually saying, you will realize that maybe the only thing that needs to be communicated is "I'm lonely; I want to spend more time with you."

I encourage all of my friends to write, especially artists. Writing down your raw thoughts on one or two pages every day can completely change your life and your art. It's one of the simplest, private ways to express everything without hurting anyone. Some people feel like they cannot write because they don't know how or they don't have anything to say. This is an excuse because the point is to express just that! If you feel like you don't have anything to say, write that until you do! There are plenty of times where I write "Ummm… I'm bored. I don't know what to say," in my journals because I literally write out my exact thoughts as I think them.

It's okay to feel pressure when you first start, but if you remain consistent, all of that will go away. You'll eventually not only write from your brain, but begin writing from your heart, and you'll see God's words right in front of you.

MEDITATION

Another way to get in-tune with yourself is by medi-tating. Meditation is the act of transforming the mind. Despite its popularity, most people complain that they can't do it, which couldn't be further from the truth. Everyone can meditate. Keep in mind that even prayer is a form of meditation. It's a personal experience, so the result is whatever you want it to be. People meditate to clear their minds, receive messages, set intentions, connect deeply with their spirit, or to find peace. There are numerous reasons to medi-tate, and no right or wrong way to do it. There are, however, techniques that are helpful to reach your desired goal.

Start by choosing a time and place to meditate where you will not be interrupted. You can either lie down or sit up straight—I prefer to lie down in bed on my back.

To begin, focus on your breath while taking deep breaths in and out. You want to make sure that you're inhaling as much air as possible through your nose and slowly exhaling it all through your mouth. As you breathe in, pay attention to how your breath feels against the hairs of your nose. You want to feel your-self become as soft as your breath.

CALM YOUR BODY

To help relax, you can do this by imagining your breath fill up every inch of your body. As you inhale, visualize your breath as an ocean wave rising through your foot, and as you exhale, see that wave crashing down at your ankles and retracting back to the bottom of your feet. On the next inhale, see that wave go just a little bit further, this time crashing at your knees and retracting to your ankles. Continue doing this until you have reached a deeper state of relaxation throughout your entire body, then begin to breathe normally. You will feel your breath become more soft, slow, and soothing.

SCAN YOUR BODY

Once you're relaxed, perform a body scan by focusing on the different body parts. Start from your feet and move up to the crown of your head. As you focus on each body part, you want to sit in this moment. You may notice a feeling of discomfort, tingling, energy, tensions, or the weight of your body part. Doing this will help you be present and sink into a deeper state of relaxation.

VISUALIZATION

You can do this especially when you need to feel peace. Imagine yourself in a place (real or imagined) that makes you feel safe and comfortable. Make it as detailed as possible and become familiar with this space so you can always come back to it.

AFFIRMATIONS

Many people use this technique to help focus, relax, or set intentions. You can say whatever you need to help you achieve your goal for meditating. For example, some people chant the sounds associated with our chakras or repeat affirmations such as, "I am love," "I am protected," or even repeat scriptures. Find what works for you.

TIP: IGNORE PHYSICAL DISTRACTIONS

It is normal to feel a tingling sensation (almost like an itch) on your body, and you will be tempted to shift your focus towards it and rub or scratch it. Feeling this sensation means you're getting closer to your relaxed state. Do not turn your attention towards it! It's a literal and physical distraction. Instead, practice mindfulness and continue to focus on your breath as you relax deeper. To your surprise, that feeling will go away.

TIP: LET YOUR THOUGHTS FLOW

Another experience you may have is thinking "too much." A myth some people have of meditation is that you're supposed to quiet your thoughts, and not think. The truth in this statement is that you do want to quiet your mind. However, if you happen to have a thought, you allow it to pass through you, rather than procreate another one. For instance, if you happen to begin thinking about what you're going to eat for lunch, allow yourself to have that thought and let it go. You don't want to start a snowball effect of internal chatter such as:

"I'm hungry for lunch. Ooo, I have leftovers in the fridge. Ugh, but I kinda don't want leftovers. Ooo, I'ma go to Chick-fil-A later. Dang, but it's Sunday. Ugh, okay fine, then maybe I'll just eat the pasta in the fridge. Oh crap, aren't I supposed to be meditating?"

At this point, you've completely shifted your focus towards your thoughts, disrupting the process of tuning into your highest self. When you find yourself getting distracted, simply go back to focusing on your breath. Sometimes I even tell my mind to be quiet, or to stay out of it, which helps me not to produce many thoughts.

∞

Once you've found yourself in a deep, relaxed state, depending on what your goal of mediation is, you'd begin doing it. If you're trying to find peace, you may remain in that state, and continue to relax deeper and deeper until you have reached a peaceful state. You can also imagine yourself in a place that brings you peace. If you're setting intentions, you may say affirmations, imagine what the rest of your day will be like, or envision yourself with something you want to manifest into the physical world.

There is no set time for you to meditate as some can meditate for as little as 5 minutes to as long as an hour. I do recommend that beginners try to meditate for at least five to ten minutes daily, or as often as you can to build yourself up to it.

Whatever your technique of reaching your desired state of mind is, it is beneficial to everyone to build this practice. Not only are you achieving peace of mind, but you are improving your overall well-being, practicing emotional healing, increasing self-awareness, and rebuilding your energy field. There are many times that I've meditated to raise my energy, and once I've finished, I've felt spiritually stronger. Then, as I go out into the world, I'll hear people say things like, "you're glowing," or even "your energy is so powerful." When you raise your energy, other people take notice, so much so that they can feel it too.

Lastly, if you can't seem to quiet your thoughts, or figure out what you're doing, go to good ole' "Hey YouTube" and use a guided meditation. My favorite is 'Meditations by Rasa.' She is who I meditated with when I had very little experience and helped me tune deeper into myself.

In October of 2017, I learned how to meditate from an old friend named Connor, whom I met during a 3-day work conference in LA. He first sparked my interest with his stories of his meditation experiences, spiritual encounters, and all of the books he read that enhanced his life. From there, he guided me through my first meditation which left a huge impression on me. I was still in school during this time, and since we lived in different parts of the country, I would call him over FaceTime, and he would guide me through mediation. Each time brought a new experience and feeling of being more at peace.

Fast forward to New Year's Eve of 2017. I was in Philadelphia, staying at my sister's apartment while she was out of the country. I was expecting to spend the holiday with my friends in New York, but it didn't quite work out. During this time, I was feeling very alone and lost. I went into a deep rabbit hole of conspiracies, which left me feeling like almost everything in my life was a lie, some of which included my religion. So there I was on New Year's Eve, away from my friends, away from my family—and away from God—or so I thought.

As I woke up on New Year's Day, I sat in bed and didn't know what to do. I didn't immediately pick up my phone, because I didn't want to look on Instagram and see everything I had missed out on, so I just sat there and stared at the ceiling. Eventually the thought of meditating popped into my head. I had only meditated with Conner a total of four times and still felt like I needed to be guided during my meditation. I didn't want to call him, because my energy was too low and I didn't want to intrude on his morning, so I went to good 'ole "Hey YouTube" and found a video that stood out to me. I had no expectations or desired outcomes from this meditation, I just went for it.

I started off taking my usual deep breaths in and out. About 10 minutes in, I was completely relaxed and felt the most at peace I had ever felt in my entire life. I listened to her tell me to relax deeper and deeper, and before I knew it, I found my body to be completely relaxed, so much so that it felt like I was spiritually somewhere else.

Later in the meditation, I found myself in the presence of angels sending me their love and energy. After feeling lonely for several months and especially at that moment on New Year's Day, their presence cleared all of my emptiness. It felt so beautiful, and I knew it was so real that I began to cry. I felt like I found God again.

This was my first spiritual encounter and still one of the most beautiful memories I have to date. This moment opened my eyes to a whole new world that my soul knew very much about, but my logical brain knew very little of. From this moment on, my life drastically changed for the better.

Overall, my spirituality has grown immensely since practicing meditation. I've found clarity within myself and have grown to know more about who I am. I've received several messages from God and healed my body through meditation. Meditation is a great tool to use as you walk through all phases of life to simply reconnect with yourself and with God. It's not as beneficial to only meditate when you need something, but it's a great tool to use as you walk through all phases of life.

FASTING

Another great way to get in-tune with yourself is by fasting. The purpose of doing so is to become more connected with your inner being. It's especially good for you if you are trying to gain clarity. In the process of fasting, you are getting rid of the toxins in your body so that you can have a clear mind, body, and spirit. You will begin to have more clarity in your visions, thoughts, and messages from God. Everything becomes heightened! Keep in mind, this is an act of faith and requires much discipline and self-control.

When you carve out earthly things, you make room for God. Rather than focusing on your physical needs, you are now more tuned in to your spiritual needs and are more susceptible to undergoing a spiritual transformation. Many people may fast for health or religious reasons, and I do think it's important for you to have a specific reason for doing so. You don't have to have super specified expectations, but it is good to be intentional so that you can make the most of your experience.

Also, be aware that your spiritual fast is personal. Fasting is not a public display of your diet, discipline, or devotion. It is a time where you and God have an intimate moment alone. In an era where we tend to overshare, it may be tempting to show others how "spiritual" you are, but please, your fasting diet is not a flat tummy tea ad. Keep it between you and God. The spiritual benefits of fasting await those who embark on their journey with humility. Know that this journey is personal to you and God. Now, after you've finished fasting, you might feel compelled to share your testament with others, and you should, as well as encourage them to embark on their own journey if needed.

I grew up in a Baptist church, where every Spring, I'd hear about fasting and Lent. Back then, my understanding of fasting was limited. I knew I was supposed to give something up, pray, and read my Bible, but I never did. It wasn't until the summer of 2017 when I was living my post-graduate life trying to figure out how I was going to move to Los Angeles that I would understand. A friend of mine told me about his decision to do the Daniel's Fast and suggested that I do it with him. I desperately needed guidance, so I agreed.

I started the Daniel Fast and unlike my childhood fast, I was actually taking the time to read my Bible and share intimate moments with God through prayer. Every conversation was different, but one of the things that remained constant was my asking for clarity and direction—my purpose for fasting. Day three changed my life forever. This is the day that

God told me everything I needed to do in life. All of these ideas came to me while meditating. I was so inspired, I hurried to jot them down and couldn't believe I was going to accomplish all of these things in my lifetime. I mean, I knew I was destined for greatness, but I didn't know what all of my greatness looked like (I still don't). During the rest of my fast, I had several other moments of inspiration and became completely immersed in my creative energy. All I wanted to do was create because so many different things were inspiring me.

My fast lasted nine days, and by the end, I felt so much lighter and clear of any negativity or self-doubt. I had also become more in tune with my body than ever before. I knew exactly when my body didn't like something I ate, and I could tell the moment I was full, and I knew what I wanted to eat at all times. It seems as though being in tune with your body is such a difficult concept to grasp, but it's really not. When your body is telling you that you are hungry—eat! When your body is telling you that you are tired—sleep! When your body is in pain—figure out why and seek healing! The whole idea is to nurture yourself and treat yourself just as you would a child. You wouldn't make a three-year-old starve or go hours and hours without sleep, so why treat your adult body that way?

My experience is just one testimony of the wonders of fasting to get closer to God. It's always good for gaining clarity and getting in-tune with your divine spirit. Going on a fast re-ignited my desire to live by faith rather than sight, which is something I encourage us all to work towards.

NATURE

Another way to tune in to ourselves is by tuning in to nature. I'm sure we can all relate to feeling a sense of renewal and purity when we're surrounded by nature. We feel more relaxed, sometimes more energized, and more grateful to be alive—but why? There is a presence of a powerful purity that affects us all because it comes directly from the source of life that is within us.

We must all recognize and understand that we are not separate from nature, but an integral part of it. While we may see nature as our environment, it is a part of our very being. The same water that fills the ocean is the same water that is in our bloodstream. The same fire that lights the sun is the same fire that heats our body. The same minerals and nutrients found in nature are the very same substances that build our body. Even the oxygen we breathe shows the symbiotic relationship between humans and plants, where both provide the necessary element for the other to live and thrive.

We are all created in harmony with nature—the most pure and divine creation. When we move towards creation, we move towards our inner selves and God. Also, being surrounded by nature has so many benefits including: stress reduction, creative boosts, an increase in sleep quality and emotional health. Through meditation and physically experiencing outdoors, we can naturally connect with our extended body, which is our world.

Through my spiritual growth, I've found my fascination of the stars and sky grow. The vast and alluring cosmos have somehow helped guide me along my spiritual path.

When I admire the sun, moon, and stars shining, I essentially feel like I am seeing something that is already within me. I also feel a sense of protection and reassurance that God is with me.

If we open ourselves up enough, we can all experience the pureness of nature and activate our natural being. When this happens, we feel peace, love, and fulfillment. This is why when we feel like we need a vacation, we always want to go somewhere surrounded by nature, whether that be water, forest, or desert. When we return home from vacation, we feel like "blah." That's because the real return home is actually to our vacation destination in nature, rather than where we spend our day to day lives.

I truly believe that what we ultimately long for is to be in tune with our inner nature—our highest self. Being immersed in a pure environment can be a great support to that process. It catalyzes a process that helps us naturally experience our true selves. Our appreciation for nature grows so much because we recognize its purity and authenticity. We begin to see ourselves in nature and gain the understanding that we too, can just *be*.

When we are in tune, we have our radio turned on and tuned in to our specific station. We begin to get in tune with the natural world, with others, and with ourselves. When we are in this state of alignment, we pass the broadcast on to others. Our hearts open, our minds clear, we begin to remember and interpret our dreams, and our intuition strengthens. We are also more aware of how our thoughts, words, and actions affect us, others, and the environment. We become more sensitive to signs and nudges from God, and we can hear God speak to us. Hearing God can come in multiple forms—meditation, intuition, and one of my personal favorites, universal signs.

IV. FOLLOW THE SIGNS

Is there such a thing as a coincidence, or does everything happen for a reason? Growing up, my mom always told me that everything happens for a reason, and when "ironic" things would happen, I'd think, "Oh wow, what a coincidence!" For instance, I'd think about someone, then they'd call me, or I'd run into them. Now that I'm older and much wiser, I understand what these moments really mean. Those coincidences are never just coincidences. *Why* they happen is for you to determine. You may not always know the reason, and sometimes finding the reason isn't that significant at that moment. The key is to simply pay attention. The more aware you become of all the signs that are given to you in life, the more understanding you will have of every "coincidence" that follows.

SYNCHRONICITY

Reality is not random. Everything is working together beyond what you can even imagine. When we experience a series of events that seem to be coincidental, we are experiencing synchronicity. Synchronicities are the stepping stones to and within the path of your destiny. They help guide us to let us know that we are in the right place at the right time, to send us messages, or to let us know we are not alone.

We all experience it, but don't give it as much attention as we should. For example, have you ever been thinking of someone, and all of a sudden, they randomly text you? Synchronicity. Have you ever been watching TV and having a conversation, and suddenly you hear the TV saying the exact same thing you just said? Synchronicity. When these events occur, we're always stunned or surprised in disbelief. Then the more we think about it, the more we realize that such perfectly choreographed events cannot happen randomly. It's as if something deep within us is suddenly activated, making us more aware of what could possibly be going on in the supernatural.

Whether we are curious or amused by these events, we awaken to the idea that something is happening and want to find the deeper meaning behind it all. There can be several reasons as to why you experience synchronicity. It could be revealing an answer to a question you may have, giving you the guidance you may have been seeking, or telling you to act on something you may have been thinking about doing.

Even though I'm aware of these moments, I am still taken aback, because they serve as such powerful confirmations. They confirm that angels are watching over me, as well as the power of the mind and tongue. It can be viewed in the same way as the law of attraction— what you put thought and energy towards will manifest in physical form. When I put energy towards thinking of someone, I'm essentially sending out vibrations that are attracting their presence in my life.

These synchronicities aren't always quick, as I've had moments that have spanned for months at a time. For example, for five months, the shows I would binge on Netflix would directly relate to my life and my relationships. It was mind-blowing how synchronized these moments were. You know how you would be in church and you feel like the pastor is speaking DIRECTLY to you? That's how I felt while innocently watching TV and would always think, "Well dang, tell me about myself then" and go reevaluate my life.

It's moments like these that are so subtle, yet so significant—if you want them to be. The more you put your awareness on these events, the more they occur. It's always going to be you, and only you, that can really find the meaning behind what it is you're experiencing. Once you do, you'll be able to make more guided decisions while walking on your divine path.

SETBACKS, DETOURS, DELAYS & RANDOM EVENTS

Often, we experience setbacks and delays in our lives and get frustrated. There are many times where I've wondered, "Why can't life just let me be great?" Then as I continue to move forward in life and look back, hindsight reveals that what I thought was a setback was really just a set up for a stronger comeback. I'm sure you or someone you know has been in a situation where something that you thought was holding you back was actually protecting you from encountering something far worse.

For example, my mom is a very organized and routine-oriented type of person. I know this from having to always clean up my room for her sake. One day she was going to work as she usually does, and for some reason, she couldn't find her car keys anywhere, despite her habit of putting them in the same place every day. She looked through her purse and everywhere around the house until about fifteen minutes later she found them. She then left the house and raced to work, only to end up stuck in traffic. Come to find out, the traffic was due to a severe car accident that had just taken place on her route to work. Had she been driving approximately fifteen minutes earlier; it's possible that she could have been involved in the accident.

It's moments like these, where God may be holding us back from where we think we ought to be to protect us from being where we don't need to be. If you're experiencing what may seem like a delay or detour in life, it's a good opportunity to assess what's really going on and choose to go with the flow of life rather than against it. This is not to say that when you're in a tough situation, you should be complacent. It's about not getting in the way and aligning yourself with where God wants you to be. It's allowing the waves of life to move you, rather than trying to swim against them.

RANDOM THOUGHTS OR URGES

As mentioned before, our emotions provide guidance to let us know if we are aligned with our true desire. We must understand this, so we can start using our emotions to our advantage rather than a catalyst to victimhood. Our feelings are more than just indicators of how emotional we are; they give us understanding and guide us with signs. Understanding my emotions helped me realize how important it was for me to start my women's organization, ALCHEMY.

I first had the idea in late February of 2019 and thought nothing of it. Actually, I did have thoughts about it, but they were rooted in fear and doubt. The thought process went something like this:

"Ooo, it would be dope to have an intimate setting with a group of young black people to talk about some real life shit."

"Mmm, and only women."

"Ehh… but who would come?"

"…who would even listen to me?" "Alright, never mind."

During this time in my life, I felt very lonely. Not in the sense that I wanted to be cuddled up with some dude, more like, I'd rather be doing cute shit with girls. However, all my close friends lived everywhere in the country except Los Angeles. The most I could do was FaceTime, which didn't quite live up to the ideal "hot girl summer" agenda, so I spent many moments to myself.

One weekend I was hanging out with Dani, one of my good friends from Howard University that had recently moved to Los Angeles. After a full day of day-partying, we went to dinner at one of my favorite places, Cafe Gratitude. We had a great chat about moving forward in life, growth, and what we wanted to work towards. For some reason I told her about my idea to start a women's event series where young, black women in Los Angeles could be vulnerable, connect, and support each other. Her response was, "Do that shit!" She then proceeded to tell me her experience of going to a women's circle in D.C. that helped her and how the vibe felt very genuine, pure, and safe.

After our conversation, I felt more confident about the idea, but it was still something I wasn't sold on, so I put it in the back of my mind. The very next day I woke up and the first thing on my mind was the women's event. I thought it was a bit strange that I was still thinking about it, but I didn't pay too much attention and brushed it off. Literally 30 minutes later I found myself in a daze envisioning how the event would look and feel. It didn't take long for me to feed into it and start brainstorming on all the cute details that I would intentionally incorporate to make the event special.

I found myself getting really excited and worked-up over what was just an abandoned idea less than 48 hours ago. I did not intend to be as excited as I was because it was distracting me from doing work at my job. Anytime I'd think about the event, I'd get excited and have a strong urge to have a whole brainstorming session on how I could make the event stimulating, safe, and inviting. "What would I talk about first?" "What would I even call it?" This unfamiliar sense of excitement and anticipation lasted for three days straight of only thinking about executing something I'd never thought I'd be doing.

During this time of my life, I was reading *Ask and It Is Given* by Esther and Jerry Hicks. I wanted to put into practice what I was reading so I tuned in to my emotions. It didn't take me long to recognize that my emotions were telling me something my logical brain couldn't seem to admit: this was something that I needed to be doing. This is what was going to nourish me in the way I long desired. It was going to grant me the close connections I wanted to have with women as well as allow myself and others the opportunity to let go of the past, and grow with one another towards a divine future. I learned from my emotions that my overwhelmingly positive feelings from this idea meant that I was aligned with my true desire. It was a sign, and gave me confirmation that this was something that I needed to act on to walk on my divine path.

Your emotions may not always paint the clearest picture; however, you can't deny their existence. The more awareness you have, the more you're able to tap into your truest feelings that will always move you towards your destiny. I'm sure you've heard of the saying, "If you want to make God laugh, tell him your plans." Well, when you can tune into your intuitive emotions, you will see the signs of where God is trying to take you, and in hindsight, you will laugh along.

DREAMS = MESSAGES

God is always present and always communicating with us, whether we realize it or not. When asking God for a sign, don't only search for it in your waking state of life. Pay attention to your life in your dreams as well, because they serve as messages. They give us a greater understanding of ourselves and allow the spirit world to penetrate our subconscious mind. Dreaming is how we align ourselves with our spirit.

To simply survive, we have to sleep. Not only to give our body rest but to break away from the limitations of the physical world and freely explore other dimensions and realities within our dreams.

For everyone who says they don't dream—you do, you just don't remember them. It's like hearing God talk to you. Some say they have never experienced this or have never had that gut feeling, but that could result from choosing to ignore it or simply not being aware of it.

While having the dream is important within itself, you must be able to recall the dream so that you can internalize and interpret the messages given to you. One way of receiving the messages embedded in our dreams is to practice recollecting them. The best way to do this is by getting in the habit of writing them down first thing every morning, before you check your phone, get up to pee, or brush your teeth. Getting into this practice will allow you to remember your dreams better and receive the messages God is trying to give to you.

I've had vivid, bizarre, and supernatural dreams since childhood, so I've been forced to pay attention to them. When I was around seven years old, every now and then, I would have dark dreams that would wake me up screaming. No one really understood what I was going through and thought it was just a nightmare, and at that age, so did I.

Eventually, those dreams slowed up, and I began to have repetitive dreams. I always dreamed of being in the same space, doing the same thing, and maybe one thing would be different. Even within my dream, I felt like I was having déja vu.

My dreams felt so real and were repetitive, so I decided to try to find a pattern. When I was a freshman in high school, I would sit in the cafeteria where we all waited before going to first period, and pull out my journal to write out my dreams, but I couldn't decipher any meaning to them. As I grew into my adult life, and my spirituality grew, I began to have more understanding of what my dreams were trying to tell me.

There have also been times when I don't have to interpret my dreams because they will blatantly speak to me. One night I had a dream that spoke to me and said, "Just be yourself." Upon waking up from that dream, I had risen right before my alarm was set to go off. It seemed like perfect timing. The next night, I had a dream and heard a voice that spoke clear as day and said, "All you have to do is be yourself, and good things will come your way." I woke up in the most peaceful way and thought, "Wow, that's crazy, I received that same message yesterday and woke up before my alarm." Literally right after I said that to myself, my alarm went off. Coincidence?

I've also had vivid dreams that have been warnings. For the span of a few months, I kept having dreams of my ex trying to kill me. Initially I thought it was weird, but it became alarming when my dad called to tell me that he had a similar dream. I eventually began to understand that those supernatural terrors were warning signs to remove him from my life to prevent him from killing me emotionally, spiritually and mentally.

Although my dreams have been spread across the spectrum of understandable to confusing, most of them have conveyed messages whether I immediately understood them or not. They are given through settings, colors, or a specific situation I've encountered in my dreams. However they are communicated to you in your dreams, you have to pay attention to them and what they may symbolize or reflect in your waking life.

If you begin to notice the patterns occurring, it's important to write them down and find out what they mean. Another option is to ask God to reveal to you what your dream means, and you will be led to pay attention to the signs to discover the true meaning of the messages being brought to you.

NUMBERS

Another way God will reveal messages to you is through numbers. I'm sure many of us grew up seeing 11:11 and saying "Ooo, make a wish," but do you know why we said that? It's because in seeing certain numbers, there is a deeper meaning behind them. When this happens, be sure to make a note of it so you are open to understand what is being communicated to you.

MEANING OF NUMBERS

0—creation

1—beginning

2—testimony

3—highest spirituality
(mind, body & spirit as one)

4—going through trials/hardship

5—favor

6—man (ego)

7—completion

8—new beginnings

9—the end

Having an understanding of numbers and what they mean has been a huge guide for me in my everyday life. They help me make decisions, give me hints and cues about circumstances I'm unsure of, and ultimately serve as a reminder that God is always with me.

LITERAL SIGNS

Sometimes God shows up in physical signs. Billboards, pictures, store signs, even street signs. There have been numerous times I've been unsure about something, and God will put a sign in my face to reveal the answer. Even times when I've been wary of something, I'll see a sign from God and immediately feel a sense of comfort wash over my body.

As I was looking for a new apartment, I was eight days away from my lease coming to an end, and I had no new place to stay. I started thinking, "Wow, so this is it… I'm going to be homeless. This is really the Los Angeles struggle I have to live. Has my time finally come?" I was obviously being dramatic. Then my mom called me to get the update on my apartment search. I had just received news that a place I applied for was rented to someone else. After I told my mom the news, I told her not to worry because I know I have people watching over me.

She responded saying, "Yes! Jesus and the angels in heaven." Shortly, I got off the phone with her, and literally a minute later, as I'm driving back home, I see a license plate that reads "4RK4NGEL." My mind instantly processes it as "ark angel" formerly known as archangel.

I had heard of this word from church, but I wasn't quite sure what it meant exactly. I looked up what it meant, and it read: an angel of high rank. This supernatural experience gave me so much comfort and confirmation that everything I believed was true, as well as what my mom told me. Angels were watching over me, and they were letting me know things would be alright.

There are also times when God will use family, friends, or even strangers to send a sign or message. I'm sure we've all experienced a stranger walking up to tell us something that we needed to hear at that moment. Or they'll start a conversation around a topic that we want to know more about or was just talking about. Moments like these don't just happen by coincidence. Your thoughts, desires, and beliefs will manifest into physical form for you to witness.

Something valuable that I realized is that everyone can be your "guru" if you listen closely. There is always guidance available to us, and the answers will always come to the questions we pose. Cultivating trust in our intuition and paying attention to the subtle, yet emphatic signs from God will enhance the journey of our lives.

If we listen, pay attention, and follow the signs, we may be led to more clarity. If we don't pay attention, then we may end up being distracted onto other paths that may not serve us. Following signs means listening for a deeper knowing and a feeling that goes with it. It may be the distinct feeling of flowing with life with ease and acceptance. Or, it may be the feeling that you need to wake up and get back on track. Even if the journey seems rough, a path connected to synchronicity has a higher potential to serve our whole self—body, mind, and heart.

V. EGO

When you decide to walk on your divine path, living as the most authentic version of you, many people will challenge you for doing so, and your ego will be triggered. Our ego is our own construction of our identity of self. It is who we *think* we are rather than who we really are. It shapes our beliefs around our personality, physical appearance, talents, experiences, relationships, etc.

We have not been conditioned by society to believe we are spiritual beings. Very often, we grow up seeing ourselves only as the person we see in the mirror. I now know that my identity goes far beyond my physical body, and while I know this to be true, there are still times where I have to remind myself because I can get caught up in the thoughts that derive from my ego. Some of which can include:

"I'm such a smart person."

"I look better than most people." "I look worse

than most people." "I'm not photogenic."

"I'm so mature for my age."

"Not enough people saw me wearing this outfit, so I will wear it again."

"I need to be successful so people will love me."

The ego hides behind the "I" and "me" in those thoughts and statements about identity. It separates us instead of allowing us to see everyone as equals. It forces us to categorize everything, making greater and lesser people, experiences, thoughts, places, and emotions. It also serves as a survival mechanism that seeks out safety and security, so when our ego feels like it is being attacked, it is relentless in defending itself. This is usually the reason why we "act out," which can look like getting into arguments or physical altercations. We feel the need to defend ourselves by proving ourselves to one another. Every thought that originates from our ego only appears as real because of how our ego perceives the world. It can be quite challenging for someone who isn't fully awakened to understand the difference between what is ego and what is really them.

WE BUILD OUR EGO

There are so many factors that cause us to live by our ego, one of those being through encouragement.

When we are encouraged to do something, our ego can be in agreement without feeling defensive. When we are not being judged, our egos are not being triggered. When we feel accomplished, our egos feel more empowered.

One of the primary ways our ego is boosted is when we receive compliments. Our ego is directly correlated to our self-esteem, so when we hold ourselves in high regard, we build confidence. We often do this through social media by showing the world our best moments in life, our best photo out of 100, our best angles, and our best captions. We receive instant gratification from the likes, comments, and engagement, which builds up our ego by being "likable" or who we think we should be.

WE BREAK OUR EGO

Our pride is dependent on how our ego perceives our worth, confidence, and self-esteem. When we experience something that affects us negatively, we can find ourselves dwindling in a spiral of insecurity and fear. The easiest way to be triggered by your ego is for there to be disagreement with who you believe you are. Most of us identify ourselves based on our ego, and when someone or something happens, that says otherwise, we feel triggered.

For instance, when we receive criticism that we can't handle, our ego is hurt. Not because we can't handle what is being said to us, but mainly because we don't agree. It's the inner conflict that we experience that creates confusion and stirs up anger inside of us.

When we fail to meet our own standards, we experience a knock to our ego. We romanticize "success" and when we are not living the life we imagined, we begin to question ourselves and our worthiness. We begin to doubt our abilities which in turn lowers our self-esteem. When I graduated from Howard University, I thought I would be living my best life. In the first few months of moving to Los Angeles, my ego was bruised. It was telling me to be disappointed in myself because I wasn't living the life I thought I should be living. My confidence was low, and I couldn't fully enjoy what was once my dream because it didn't look how I imagined it would.

Rather than just embracing my life at that moment and really enjoying the journey, I tried to act like I wasn't struggling financially, emotionally, or mentally. There was a lot of inner conflict with what my ego would tell me about my life, what my spirit had me believe about my life, and what I was actually experiencing in my life.

It didn't help that my colleagues on social media

seemed to be living their best lives; while, I was struggling in LA trying to make a dollar. Social media is one of the easiest ways to build or break your ego. It's very easy to accept what you see on social media for what it portrays, then fall in the trap of comparing your situation to others. Instagram allows people to create fairy-tale façades of their lives when in actuality, you don't know what's not being shared from those who seem to be living a "perfect" life. They could be going through family issues, health issues, who knows? However, your ego will encourage you to compare online images to your life and make their situation about you.

WE COMPARTMENTALIZE EGO

As previously mentioned, ego separates and categorizes everything. So if my ego undergoes experiences that lead it to believe I am one thing, it is then difficult for me to express myself as anything else. For example, if my ego tells me that I am a beautiful woman, I am compelled to carry myself consistent with the way I believe a beautiful woman would behave. When in reality, there is no such thing as *how* a beautiful woman is supposed to behave.

The ego will compartmentalize every experience, relationship, and feeling you have, forming an identity around you to serve as reference and protection. This is why it's so uncomfortable to introduce ourselves as something other than what our ego labels us as, because we would expose our raw, and pure spirit. We then hide behind the shell of our egos to protect ourselves from experiencing what we perceive as danger when in actuality, it is beautiful and liberating.

WE ACT OUT OF EGO

Our actions derive from two different places: true self and ego. When we act out of ego, we only lessen our living experience for our true being. It's in situations of uncertainty, fear, or anger when our ego thrives. Our ego arises when it feels the need to be shielded from someone or something. This leads us to express "cover emotions," which derive from the mind rather than the heart.

We also act out of ego when we decide who is and who isn't worthy of love and proceed to act accordingly. It's one of the reasons people favor attractive people. Ego says, "they are physically attractive, so they are worthy of love and friendship" or "being friends with them will make me look better." It's all ego, and it isn't solely from the heart. So we find ourselves going after people, conditions, or material items in life because our ego says, "This will be a good look."

If you see someone that physically appeals to your ego, you may think, "I have to get to know them." You then pursue them and either experience an ego boost because you got their number or experience an ego break because you got rejected. This only results in you acting out of ego even more. Especially if your ego hasn't been satisfied, it now has to compensate for that hurtful experience.

Oftentimes we allow hurtful experiences that derive from pleasing our ego to accumulate and make more egotistical decisions rooted from this painful place. If we get rejected for a job, we think, "well maybe I'm not qualified" or "maybe I should apply for a lower position." If we get rejected by a love interest, we start to think:

- "Well maybe I'm not attractive enough."
- "If only I had more money or better clothes, more people would be attracted to me."
- "Maybe I should lose/gain more weight."
- "Maybe I should make myself seem less available to be more desirable."

We try to rationalize the outcome of acting out of ego and convince ourselves to accept an outcome that we don't want or deserve. We want love, but how can we expect to receive love if our actions aren't rooted in love?

In order to deal with conflicts and problems in life, we use a range of defense mechanisms to feel better about ourselves. When the ego is threatened, we will do anything to strengthen our self-esteem. We all have a desire to feel successful and accomplished, and if anything happens to threaten us, we act out.

When we were kids and would get teased about the clothes our parents dressed us in, having an out-of-place tooth, being too skinny or too fat, we felt threatened and ultimately less worthy. This often results in why we yell, bully, and are violent towards one another. It's because we feel we have to take away someone else's power to gain power of our own. Our ego believes that gaining this power will fill a void and put us on the path to our personal definition of success.

If you believe success is having power, your ego is going to make it your mission to always have power. When anyone or any circumstance makes you feel like power is being taken from you, you will likely go into defense mode and do or say anything to get your power back. You'll find yourself fighting for it in any circumstance which can lead to unhealthy relationship patterns.

Don't fall into the trap of succumbing to an egotistic response—instead, check your ego, know your true self, be understanding, and don't take everything personally. When you try to find understanding for another person, you put the brakes on a tendency to only care about yourself.

The ego's voice is much louder than the voice of your true self, so you must pay close attention to your more enlightened counterpart. It's really simple; we all want to love and be loved. However, our ego feeds on the fear of revealing these desires and not receiving them back. To react and act with your highest self, focus on what's in the now. Don't concern yourself with possible perceptions, uncertain outcomes, or the ways you may fall short. Focus on what's around and inside of you.

Our ego is simply a tool that allows us to have an identity in this world. The persona that we create is not permanent because it can be changed and molded, while our true self—our core essence, remains permanent and unchanged. Just as a chameleon changes colors to blend with its environment, we change our personality or manners in various social settings to fit the circumstance. However, no matter how many times a chameleon changes colors, it remains a chameleon. No matter how many times we change our personality, mind, or manners, we are still the same soul that lives inside. The important thing is to be self-aware and clear that your ego is the tool and not the master. There is only one true master: the God within.

EGO DEATH

We are all born from the same consciousness, only knowing love and compassion for others. However, at an early age, we are taught that our worth lies in other people's opinions. This pushes us to seek attention, love, and acceptance outside of ourselves, which then forces us to operate on the terms of our ego. So, how can we start living through our higher, more conscious self? Honestly, it's a commitment that won't transpire overnight and takes consistent practice, but there are great benefits from transcending your ego.

When we remove egotism, we uncover our humility. While some may define humility as low self-esteem, I see it as being emotionally neutral. It's an attitude where we don't need to put ourselves above others, but we don't put ourselves below them, either. We have confidence in ourselves yet recognize that everyone makes a contribution. You don't feel the pressure to live up to someone else's expectations, and you don't feel others have a need to live up to yours. When you value your sense of self-worth, it's easier to have confidence in yourself and appreciate others, because you don't need or expect anything from them. So rather than behaving from our emotions, we can move and react from a sense of purpose.

Knowing and understanding your purpose in life will keep you from falling into the trap of seeing the world through the perspective of the ego. We all have something we want to accomplish, change, or create in some form. The journey of becoming who we think we should be is usually a long marathon with many obstacles testing us along the way. Without connecting to a higher sense of purpose, we're easily susceptible to being triggered if ego is the only thing that sustains us.

Ego tells us that our meaning comes from our accomplishments and power over others, and that material possessions will bring us fulfillment. Spirit tells us that we are perfect and accomplished just as we are, no matter what we accomplish in this lifetime. We grow more confident when we have a clear understanding that we use our talents, skills, and abilities in ways that bring us pure satisfaction within the heart.

The death of the ego isn't truly a death, as it will

always be a part of us. Instead, it's more like a transcendence as we evolve beyond the shackles of our ego and leave it behind. When we live beyond its negative influence, we return to our true nature. This experience can be both beautiful and terrifying, depending on how ready we are to let go of ego. For some, this loss of identity can be a terrifying experience, because the ego's defense mechanism kicks in to keep itself attached. But for others, the death of the ego is just another step on a lifelong path of spirituality.

My ego death began when I started to live beyond the means of my self-centered thoughts and, in turn, my whole life changed. I started encountering omens that led me down a deeper path of heightened spirituality. One of my favorite books is called, *Be Here Now* by Ram Dass. He talks about undergoing an ego death, and what's funny is that he mentions they are looking for volunteers.

As traumatic and uncertain as a spiritual awakening can be, if you're in this profound shift, you need to add intention to the new you that you want to bring into the world. Re-birthing yourself is part of the process. Everything gets re-birthed so that you can come into alignment with truth, love, and eternity while leaving the past behind.

VI. LIVING IN THE PAST

WHY WE DO IT

There are moments where I can lose myself in a daze because I spend so much time thinking about my past. I try to dress it up by calling it "self-reflection" or "self-analyzation," but all I'm doing is reliving what has already occurred. Well, even though I know I should move on from these moments, my heart isn't always ready to. I have a past full of beautiful memories that have been painted with pain. Like most people, I have suffered the loss of people close to me, I have been manipulated, and I have experienced a persistent feeling of loneliness.

Obviously, not all of my past is painful; sometimes I like to think about what was, because what used to be can sometimes feel better than what is. I'll think about the times when things were more simple.

All of those moments are easy to get lost in because they're familiar and comfortable. It's often easier to think about the past because sometimes it's easier than facing reality. It's easier to reminisce about a relationship when it was just beginning than it is to actually deal with your current relationship problems. Everything has already happened, so unlike the present, there aren't any surprises in the moment. The script has already been written, and there's nothing we can do to change it.

Often, we immerse ourselves in unnecessary worry with our fear of the unknown. Most of us think of all the worst things that could happen to prepare ourselves mentally, emotionally, and physically for "what if" moments. Additionally, in an effort to be helpful, other people will project their fears onto us with warnings from their assumed "what if" moments. In turn, we suffocate ourselves with probabilities instead of allowing ourselves to breathe in the beauty of the now. It's great to reflect and to plan ahead, but we should not be a prisoner of what has or hasn't already happened. Our past will guide us to new obstacles, experiences, and lessons, so it's important that we use our past as a tool to help us plan for the future and make better decisions in the moment.

When we find ourselves still harping on the past and filling ourselves up with regret, we only hold ourselves back. I'm sure there's plenty of times where you've found yourself re-playing an altercation you had with someone, or even thinking about an old relationship. You spend so much time thinking about what you should've done or pondering if you made the right decision? Who was wrong?

Who was right? We accumulate this information, and with the help of our ego, we judge ourselves to validate our actions and feelings from the past. When we sit wondering if we fit in those constraints, we fail to live in the moment and find ourselves living in the past.

Over the years, I've come to realize that the past is gone. It no longer exists. Yes, you have a memory of it, but it's ultimately gone. Done. Finito. Never coming back. You can do what you can to cope with it, but none of that will make a difference in the present truth. When you wake up and realize that the magic in life is happening right now— you will feel SO liberated. Yet, as complex humans, we make it so much more complicated than it needs to be.

WHY IT'S REGRESSIVE

Without even realizing it, most people are content with a growth-avoidant life. They are okay with things staying the same and living with what's familiar to them. We are all guilty of doing this in so many areas of life. We stay in jobs, cities, and relationships knowing we need to walk away, but we stay because it's familiar and comfortable.

When you choose to stay in your comfort zone, knowing deep down, you need to move, it becomes distracting and disruptive for your growth. Had I decided to go to college in what was familiar to me, my hometown of Houston, Texas, I would not have met more than half of the people I now know by attending Howard University in Washington, D.C. I would not have experienced so many other cultures, backgrounds, and perspectives. By stepping outside of my comfort zone, I became enriched by the experience. The best things in life are always there, waiting for us to decide to step into our destiny to receive them.

We can't move on and grow if we're still living as the same person we once were. We allow past situations to control present moments by carrying the weight of old narratives. They vary all across the board from "I'm unworthy of love," "I can't do this," or "I can never forgive this person." One of the narratives that I lived by was that I was a newly introvert. Around my junior year of college, I became very shy and private, which hindered me from building relationships with my colleagues. Here and there, when I felt comfortable to show up as myself, I would hear my peers express how shocked they were at how sociable I actually was. I attributed it to not being an outgoing person, and felt satisfied continuing to live that myth.

It wasn't until after I moved to LA that I decided to change. Well, technically, I was forced to change. I had no real friends or family there so unless I was going to fall into the realms of depression, I needed to socialize and make friends. First, I stopped telling people that I was an introvert because I wanted to stop believing it and speaking it into existence. That lie I told myself was simply an excuse to give others so they wouldn't expect me to reveal more of my true self. Then, I had to push past the internal boundaries of comfortability that were safe but equally damaging and limiting. I found power in honoring my authentic self in the moment, which I learned doesn't exclusively abide by either label of introvert or extravert.

That exercise helped me realize the power of the

mind and tongue. The longer I believed and spoke of a myth I no longer wanted to bear, the longer it would remain true. Even when I spoke of not being a shy and private person with the desire to change, I was still validating an old narrative.

We often tell ourselves we are something that we once were and then look for confirmation. As we evolve into wiser and lighter beings, we sometimes forget to acknowledge the growth we've achieved. Oftentimes we don't see the inner work we've done. Other times we're insecure about our greatness and are afraid of who we will become once we step into our power. It can be easier for us to see ourselves as who we've been rather than who we are becoming, especially if the person we once were resulted from trauma.

It is difficult to move on from traumatic experiences. Without realizing it, you can find yourself reacting to current occurrences in a certain way because of past traumas. You find yourself attracting people who are similar to those who've brought pain in your life and wonder why. Is it because subconsciously, you still view yourself as a victim of your pain? Take it from me; you will be much happier in life when you decide to prevent your past from controlling your present.

MY PAST

While attending University, I was in an abusive relationship. I never thought I would be in such a situation, but it happened to me. I didn't even realize I was in an abusive relationship for a long time, because it started off small and grew into a more severe situation. It began with slight pushing, each time harder than the last. I was naturally aggressive and playful, so early on I would participate and aggravate my aggressor. At five foot three, I was trying to have a pushing war with a guy that's six foot three, and I lost, every time. It only annoyed me at first, and I would get over it, way too quickly.

I never took into consideration that we were both being abusive towards each other. My partner had his own internal issues, and he always revealed his insecurities to me through violence and abuse. There were times he'd grab me by my wrist and hold them so tight I couldn't move, and if I tried to escape, he'd just tighten his grip on me to make it hurt even more.

I'd eventually find myself stuck in his room with tears streaming down my face and screaming his best friend's name to come upstairs and help me. His friend yelled from downstairs, "Y'all good?" As I'm yelling, "No, please help me!" my partner yells, "Yeah, we good!" His friend did nothing. Like many men, he chose to ignore the obvious. Being held hostage didn't leave any physical damage, it just pissed me off that he was trying to control me in such a way. Even at this stage, I didn't see my relationship as abusive.

As we were on a trip to Miami for spring break, things began to escalate. One night I was so fed up with having to deal with him that I left our Airbnb at 1 'o'clock in the morning with nothing but my phone. I didn't think anything through, I just instinctively wanted to get as far away from him as possible. He followed me outside and yelled behind my back the most degrading words I've ever heard anyone say to me. I finally realized that my partner was being verbally abusive. At that moment, I could only think, "How did I get here?" I felt crazy because I couldn't believe I was enduring this. This wasn't like me.

A year later, I found myself still associated with this guy; I was finding comfort in what was familiar. As we were waiting for an Uber to pick us up from a party, another episode started. We argued so much that our Uber driver kicked us out of the car on the side of the street. We were in the middle of nowhere in North East D.C., and all I could see were the streetlights and vacant roads. Suddenly, I felt him snatch my phone out of my hand to try to go through it. I began yelling at him to give it back while jumping my highest to reach for it. He kept pushing me away from him and moving his arm even higher and further back so that I couldn't reach it. After a few failed attempts, I tried jumping up again to grab my phone, and as I came down, my hand got caught in his chain and it broke off. In what felt like slow-motion, we both watched his chain fall in the dirt. He looked at me with hurt and rage in his eyes. Next thing I know, I felt my iPhone and his fist hit me dead in my face. I immediately gasped for air with my mouth dropped open in complete shock.

Even after dealing with him for years and seeing the red flags of abuse, I never thought it would go this far. Tears instantly fell down my face, and a small knot began to immediately grow on the side of my temple near my left eye. The first thing he said was "Wtf, this is your fault" followed with, "You should've never snatched off my chain." This moment felt like a movie to me. A familiar scene where the woman is getting abused, and you never imagine yourself ever being in that position, so you say to yourself, "Wow, this girl is dumb as hell." This time, that girl was me. I couldn't believe that this was happening to me. At this point, I never felt more powerless, vulnerable, and victimized in my life.

This experience haunted me well after it took place. It's one of the vilest memories I have to date, and it affected many relationships I built later in my life. I wasn't able to trust people the same as before, and I became skeptical about anyone who appeared to be controlling in any way. This wasn't only with romantic relationships, but with everyone. It wasn't until a year later that I could be honest with myself about having been in an abusive relationship. Once I could be honest with myself about my experience, I could begin to heal.

I was embarrassed that I allowed myself to be in and tolerate that situation, and I didn't want anyone to think of me as that same person. I couldn't move on from the pain of that relationship and I envisioned myself as still being that tolerable, naive, broken, and abused girl. I couldn't acknowledge the person who came out on the other side of having gone through that—someone who was wiser, more secure, and aware. This shame kept me in denial for a long time. Until I could admit my reality to myself, only then could I become comfortable with admitting it to others.

I honestly wish I had more courage to be more open about it then and didn't feel the need to protect my abuser. I felt so indebted to him, but for what? He literally did everything to hurt me in so many ways, so why did I care if his own actions caused him pain? Why couldn't I have left him the first time he hurt me? Maybe because people associated me with him for so long that I didn't know who I'd be without him? I was afraid of myself. I was afraid of who I'd become without him. I was afraid of my own success. It sounds strange, but yes, that's exactly what that was—afraid to be alone and face myself. After having done so, I'm glad. The real me is a person of love, and I trust myself fully.

HEALING

It's so interesting that after having gone through something troubling in our past, we immediately look at ourselves and ask, "How did I end up in this situation?" "What did I do to deserve this?" or "How could I have prevented this?" We over-analyze our previous decisions and come up with some reason as to how we could've prevented a situation. Then we move forward in life without resolution and begin acting in ways that we think will protect us from repeating our past when in reality, all we're doing is letting our past traumas control our present lives.

After I stopped feeling insecure and relieved

myself of the dead weight of my past, I realized a key lesson: what happened in my past wasn't about me. It helped me learn more about myself and taught me a lesson, but the cause of my abuse didn't have much to do with me, but a whole lot to do with my abuser. Realizing this helped me release the pressure and judgment I was placing on myself from what he did.

Furthermore, I realized that his actions weren't personal to me. Yes, while I was on the receiving end of his violence, he wasn't just abusing me—he was an abuser. There wasn't anything I did that made me deserve to be abused; it was just his accumulated insecurities, upbringing, and personal issues. By having this newfound revelation, I was able to look at other traumas in a similar way and find healing in knowing that, as much as I want to think that I am the center of everyone's universe, it isn't all about me.

While I wasn't responsible for what happened to me, I knew I was responsible for how I reacted to it. If I wanted this to be a lesson and use it to better myself, I needed to have a clear understanding of what I could control and focus on only that. I did not have control over being abused or making my abuser feel bad or apologetic for his actions. However, I did have control over how I'd let that situation affect me throughout my life. For example, if you got hit by a drunk driver and couldn't walk anymore, it wouldn't be your fault that you got hit, but it would still be your responsibility to learn how to walk again. As frustrating as the situation may be, it's your responsibility to heal, move forward, and better your life.

As mad as I was at my abuser, I knew very early on that I couldn't make him feel the way I felt—I don't even think that would be possible. Trust me, a side of me wanted to ruin his life, and I knew that I could, but what would that do for me? Would his pain take away from my pain? No, it would just remind me of my own suffering and screw-up somebody else's life in the process. It takes a lot of maturity not to want bad for someone who has done you wrong, but it's so crucial that we shift our focus to get rid of all the negative energy and hurt. Only then, can we move on and feel comfortable being vulnerable and trusting with other people again.

CHANGING YOUR PERSPECTIVE

Typically, when we're going through what feels like a low point in life, that's all we can see for ourselves. In Phase 1, it feels like the world is against us, and we're sitting in a place of darkness. We do our best

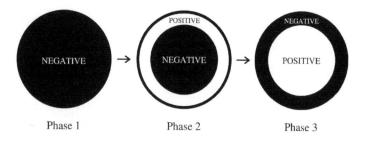

Phase 1   Phase 2   Phase 3

to push through, waiting to see the light at the end of the tunnel. When we finally move forward and look back in hindsight, we enter Phase 2 as we recognize the good that came out of that experience. This is usually where our healing stops. We acknowledge negative situations and attach positive outcomes to it.

I didn't realize that even though I was able to recognize the good that came out of my past, I was still living in it. I was still seeing "abusive relationship" as the focal point of a period in my life, and subconsciously I was still allowing it to control me. I was healing from it, but I still saw that perspective as the central part of my story. Now, that is a part of my story, but what I realized was missing, was the change of perspective. I needed to step into Phase 3, which is changing your perspective to make the positive outcome the focal point of your story and the negative situation as the details.

This next phase is important because this change in perspective allows you to see yourself as the result of something, rather than seeing yourself as a victim to your past and then sprinkling the positive glitter on top. I can now see "trusting myself" as the focal point of my past and can still be honest about the details of what got me there.

Naturally, we are magnets to our past and our imagined future. We allow everything that has happened to us or things we've seen create an illusion to guide us in life. Our thoughts, desires, actions, and words all derive from this illusion and prevent us from focusing on the present. Reflecting on past mistakes to learn is beneficial as long as lessons are learned, and you're not stuck reliving the past. Doing so just prevents us from stepping into our greatness and distracts us from the beauty right in front of us.

In the same way, when our mind travels into the future, all it does is fill us with useless anxiety over what could be but isn't. Every time our mind goes to the past or future, it is a good exercise to transport ourselves back to the present moment. The past and future only exist in our heads; the only thing that really exists is the here and now.

VII. LIVING IN THE MOMENT

"Live in the moment" has always been my go-to phrase that summarized my ideas on life. I didn't even know what it meant exactly, but I definitely had it on my Myspace page in a pink, glittery WordArt gif. I thought I was popping. As I grew older, I began to have a deeper understanding of what that meant. This whole time, I was telling myself and others to just be. Living in the moment is recognizing my past and envisioning the goals I have for the future, but focusing my mind and energy on all that is now and true. Much like the idea of taking things one day at a time, you break that down into one moment at a time, like every new breath you take.

It's when you internalize all that's happening around you, that you are able to experience the rush of being alive. Living in the now is something most of us take for granted, especially those who are young. It is because as youth, we think we're going to live a long and enduring life. If you ask anyone over 50 about life, they will likely tell you, it moves FAST!

Life is about more than experiencing a certain level of peace; it's encountering the supernatural on a daily basis. When you can tune into the now, you can see how God moves in your life. You will begin to witness miracles, have supernatural encounters, access your power, and understand the control you have over your life.

Moreover, living in the now relieves the pressure of being a picture-perfect ideal version of yourself. I know for me, I thought I had to be a version of me that was well-liked and received a certain kind of attention to feel important. To me, attention meant love, no matter what form it came in. This led me straight into a pit of toxicity that I had to work even harder to remove myself from. It was when I realized I didn't have to try, that I could simply just be. I finally recognized that all I ever wanted I found in a relationship with God. It didn't happen overnight; it took pure, quality time with myself to build this relationship and be a witness to its magic.

WHAT PREVENTS US

As simple as living in the moment sounds, it is still challenging to grasp the concept and put it into action. We get so absorbed living in the past and worrying about the future that we can't seem to appreciate what's happening in the now. We mature through life thinking we have to reach a target for money and success. We put ourselves through an emotional and egotistical obstacle course to receive love when it's right in the palm of our hands, and we don't even know it. It isn't until we stop and experience the essence of God that we can allow ourselves to be filled with the kind of love we tear ourselves apart searching for.

This isn't to shut down the idea of having goals. However, if you say to yourself, "I will only be happy if I get a million dollars," then you're placing your happiness into the future, which is never attainable because all that we have in every moment of life is now. You can't put the richness of God into a cause-and-effect scenario. There is no such thing—God just is. All the things we think we want—pleasure, money, and objects—are just earthly expressions of what we really want—love, happiness, and fulfillment. Within us already are all of those things. You don't strive for it; you simply recognize it.

Our survival relies primarily on judgment, learning, and planning. We judge our past experiences in life, and if something hurts us, we avoid walking down that same path to avoid the pain. Throughout my life, I've learned that allowing certain people to experience my love and vulnerability has caused me pain, so I've built up walls to protect myself from experiencing the hurt. I thought my distance was just good discernment, but what I was really distancing myself from was me. I wasn't allowing myself to live in the moment, because I was trapped by the pain of an old version of me. It wasn't until I allowed my past to stay in the past that I could let my current self experience new moments like a child and just *be*.

We all use our adverse emotions from past experiences to help guide us, but more times than not, they prevent us from being open to what's new and real. These emotions can be used as a tool, but if we find ourselves living in a pit of guilt, shame, and regret, we become marooned in our past. We also have to understand that we aren't always going to learn a lesson in one mistake. Sometimes it may take two, three, or even twenty times. All that matters is that we learn from them and give ourselves permission to move forward. Learning this has helped me live in the moment, and not be afraid to have new experiences because I think they could cause me pain. When we don't allow ourselves to take what we *think* are risks, we get paralyzed with fear of moving forward with our lives, which isn't living in the moment, it's avoiding the moment.

Some of us are more focused on the future. We prefer to plan things out and explore new ideas, some of which never get completed. This is another way of avoiding the moment. When we constantly live in our future vision, we neglect what's happening in the present and miss out on the richness of life. Sometimes it's because we are too focused on achieving something in the future and forget that whatever it is we are trying to obtain is already within. Other times we are simply too afraid to face the present and don't have the necessary grounding to get real with our current lives.

Our fear of the unknown cripples us from living boldly. This is what makes life beautiful, the surprise of it all, knowing that your life can change in an instant, whether good or bad. Most people only want the good and can't take the bad, but that's the duality of life. Naturally, we judge these new experiences, and no matter how strong and certain our personal beliefs are, they all derive from our perspective, which is an unreliable measure of truth, because it's limited to one's point of view. However, it seems reliable and true to us because it's all we've ever known.

Of course we can't learn without experiences from our past, and we can't make plans without thinking about the future. However, we have to divorce ourselves from the two and find a way to live in the only timeline that's alive—the now. Time is simply a social construct, but to the human mind, time is viewed as a continuous and linear process. We organize moments in our life as states, rather than continuous flows. We remember life in the third grade, middle school, senior year of high school, college years, our 20's, our 30's, and so on. If we were more aware of the continuous nature of time, we might be more able to let go of our more difficult states of consciousness and resist labeling them. We like to compartmentalize our experiences into labels so we can better understand them, but this actually takes us away from being present and experiencing the state, as not just one thing, but as many different facets of a rich and full experience.

HOW TO LIVE IN THE MOMENT

Part of the solution is to work on being present. That means using your senses to become in-tune with your spirit. Whether you sit and hum a word or phrase, focus on a candle flame, or pray, those are all actions that induce you to live in the moment. When you aren't able to complete your meditative rituals, you can simply remember to breathe. We are supernatural beings in which life is happening through us. When we bring our awareness to our breath, we are subconsciously reminded of that truth.

Every moment is unique, not like any other, despite what our mind tells us. We are not just one person with a fixed identity that remains the same throughout our entire life. We are so much more than that. We aren't who we were yesterday or last year, and we are never fixed. If we can resist identifying with earthly labels, we free ourselves to be whatever we want to be in any given moment.

Overcoming difficult times in my life is when this message was most prevalent. I'm reminded that I'm not the same person I once was, and that alone frees me to the opportunity to be present. It's a process, sometimes an uncomfortable and painful one, but if embraced, we obtain true freedom. Being in the present is about being here without trying to change anything. This is very difficult for most of us to do because we struggle to be somewhere else.

Another way to practice living in the moment

is mindfulness. This method requires focus and concentration on one thing at a time, whether it be focusing on each breath you take, an action you are performing, the step in front of you, or your thoughts. With everything that you do, think, or say, you put all of your attention towards that one thing and become aware of yourself.

For example, when you are eating, focus on every movement of your hand and every sensation and taste. From how you pick up your fork, to how heavy the fork feels, the watering of your mouth knowing something's coming in, the point in which you can feel the steam of your food condensate against your upper lip, the texture of your food, all of the spices in your food, at what point in your mouth you can taste your food the most, and so on. You treat eating as a sacred activity like it's the most important thing in the world. Everything has equal importance, so you don't feel the need to focus on anything but what you are doing at this very moment. You can utilize this method during multiple activities throughout the day. The more often you practice focusing on what's in front of you at the moment, the hidden beauty of everything begins to reveal itself to you.

∞

When you wake up in the morning, where does your focus go? What is your very first thought? Most people start their morning with a stream of mental chatter that only intensifies throughout the day. This may be the case without you even realizing it. When practicing mindfulness, you don't have to work to any degree in eliminating the mental chatter; all you have to do is be aware of it. When you become aware of your thoughts, you will notice that some of them have no real importance in your life, and you will slowly disengage.

After mastering the ability to focus intently on your thought processes and actions, the profound changes begin to occur. You can now go from thinking to doing to simply being. After seeing that your body doesn't really need your self-conscious attention or permission to operate, you will be able to let go of the focus on doing and shift into a place of just *being* with what *is*. This is when you can finally experience the profound peace you have been desiring.

I would also like to add that being doesn't exclude thinking or doing. It's not dedicating your life to live like a rock. Being is more of a higher state of consciousness. You are now in control, whereas before, you were a slave to your own mental and physical impulses. Being and living in the moment is loving, living, happiness, freedom, breathing, and simply just being. That's the beauty of us, human beings; we were created with everything we need inside of us so we could simply just be.

THE IMPORTANCE

Several benefits come from integrating these practices into your daily life, one of those being the ability to have more focus. When you live in the moment, you aren't clouding your thoughts, feelings, or experiences with anything other than what's relevant in your current state. Imagine you're shopping in the store, and your favorite song comes on. You're trying to listen to it, but you can barely hear over the loud chatter of customers talking and little kids running around. Then you remember you brought your headphones with you, so you put them on and play the same song through your phone. There's now a huge difference in the sound and clarity of the song, right? That's what living in the moment is like.

It's being able to tune out the worries of the past and the anxiety of the future to focus on the now. You're able to see and understand life more clearly when you're all the way tuned in to the moment. Life literally becomes amplified! You become more aware of universal signs. Your intuition strengthens, you start having more sureness, and ultimately make more decisions that are fulfilling to you!

You become less worried about what could go wrong with a decision you make and less troubled with the outcome. Children are able to find everything so interesting because they approach everything like it's their first time experiencing it, even if it's not. The smile on their face is so genuine and pure, unlike the average adult. When they want to stop in the middle of the street to pet a dog or cry because they want their favorite toy, they aren't thinking about anything else except what they want at that very moment. It doesn't matter what they did yesterday or even an hour ago because all they're thinking about is their satisfaction at that moment. I wonder how we would operate in a life where every day was brand new, and nothing else mattered. Who would we be if we weren't daunted with our shame of yesterday or stressed over expectations?

I've come to realize that these methods have led me to live a more fulfilling and fearless life. Oftentimes, the result of choosing to live in the moment doesn't appear until much later in my life; most times, it is instant. Living in the moment has led me to talk to the right people at the right time to get me in the right position. Living in the moment has pushed me out of my comfort zone to live out my dreams. It's living in happiness and freedom by simply just being present.

VIII. PURPOSE

I think we all yearn for personal meaning and a deeper understanding of life. That's what connects us all—our innate desire to feel connected to something larger than life. Our purpose is our driving force of existence and the reason why we continue to live. Without purpose, we would become lost, hopeless, deprived of joy, and may even feel worthless. Believe it or not, there's a reason for everything happening in this world. In my experience in life, this statement has held its weight in truth. Others believe that some occurrences are merely a coincidence and see everything as cause and effect. The perspectives are different, but the experience is the same.

I've started to become a "master manifester." I'll set intentions on how I want my day, week, or month to be, and then BOOM, it happens! I'm always amazed by the power invested in me. Other times when things occur that I didn't ask for, and there's nothing I can do about it, I ask, "Why is this happening to me, God?" It isn't until I've gone through the experience and come out on the other side that I can realize the purpose behind it all. You can look at both situations as the cause and effect of your daily actions, or as something bigger than us all. I feel the truth lies in the latter. This belief has never been a band-aid over deeper problems that need tending to; it's always been a reminder for me to have patience, see things through, and ultimately find beauty in the journey.

You don't always have to understand why something is happening at the moment. Oftentimes things will go exactly the way you planned, and other times you find yourself having no control over circumstances. Both outcomes are learning moments, and if you're like me, someone who has a desire to feel in control, guess what? Although things happen that are unplanned, you're still in control of how you react to it. This is your "free will" to God's master plan that is in store for you.

You have to want to see things through. Life is filled with twists and turns, but you have to stick around until the end. Things get better, and other times things get worse, but I can promise you there's beauty in it all. In my worst times, after I've sat in my feelings, I try my hardest to see the good in my situation, no matter how bad it seems. Something that has helped me find positivity in those moments is writing in my journal. Every morning I'd wake up, and before starting my day, I'd write what I'm grateful for. This allowed me to sit in gratitude and carry that feeling throughout the day despite my unpleasant feelings or situation. When my day was over, I'd write everything I did that day that I was proud of. Then I'd write how I could be better tomorrow. I would finish it with an encouraging note to myself as my inner spirit or my inner child. Here's an example of what my list looks like:

GRATEFUL:

- health
- good music
- family & friends/relationship with God
- creative ideas
- new opportunities
- clear skin
- living in LA

PROUD TODAY:

- working out after work
- booking headshot session
- doing full skin care routine
- brainstorming for ALCHEMY

HOW TO BE BETTER TOMORROW:

- workout
- call family
- make fresh green juice

LETTER TO MYSELF:

"Kamri, you is a Killa. The real, OG Killa Kam is coming back, but more evolved & developed & vibrating higher. I love you girl ♥."

—XOXO KAM 04.9.19

I hope this helps you to write yourself into happiness. Doing this consistently has never failed to help bring me out of dark times in my life. On a day-to-day basis, I'm usually able to maintain my happiness, but when I'm not, and have to force myself to choose happiness, this works.

A lot of times, when we feel down about something,

it's usually because things aren't going as we planned. Our life has now started to go in a different direction than we imagined, or perhaps it hasn't moved at all. However, God's timing is so divine, and when God moves, you must do so, too. I've realized this over and over again. I may have no idea how a situation will work out, but it works out… because it always does, and at the right time.

FINDING & UNDERSTANDING YOUR PURPOSE

When finding your purpose, it's easy to believe that our purpose is our passion. I can't tell you why anyone was brought to Earth, but I can assure you that your purpose is beyond your passion. A lot of people confuse the two, and it's an understandable mix-up. What I've grown to learn is that our passions and gifts are what we are created to *do*, and our purpose is what we are created *for*. You can be gifted with an amazing voice to sing; however, your purpose may be to provide healing. Those two things work hand in hand, but they are not the same.

Your purpose is a divine assignment given unto you before birth. Your passions are your gifts and talents which help facilitate you to live in your purpose. Some feel that setting the example and inspiring others to follow their dreams is their purpose and just that. That may absolutely be some people's assignment here on Earth, however, I want you to ask yourself, is it really?

Since our passions help us live in our purpose, we can't always see the bigger picture of what God is really using us for. We can get caught up in the natural world, forgetting that our purpose comes from divinity and purity, so it's beyond anything here on Earth. Sometimes we get a small glimpse of purpose, see how different it is from our expectations, and run away from it. We find ourselves operating for something else God didn't call us for. Or better yet, operating solely in our passions for the wrong reasons and becoming frustrated when we aren't rising to the next level. When we try to run away from what God has called us to do, we can't help but find ourselves disappointed and defeated time and time again.

This is usually the case when times in your life seem to never go right. When it's just one calamity after another that appears to be preventing you from moving forward in life; this is God trying to redirect you to where you're actually supposed to be. People wonder why they can't find a job but never think to wonder if they're looking for a job in the right place. You could very much be destined to work in the music industry, but if you're so busy trying to find a position to be an artist manager, you interrupt God's plan for you to become the artist.

Most of the time, what we desire deep in our hearts *is* for us. You can literally feel it because it's so true. The moment you decide to stop applying for jobs to be an artist manager and focus on being the artist you already are, you see a sharp shift happen in your life. Completing your divine assignment is something only God can help you do, and you won't be able to deny it. You start to see tables turned, rooms shaken, and all kinds of miracles that only a higher power could work just for you. There's a different kind of grace and mercy extended unto you when you're walking in your purpose.

The Alchemist by Paulo Coelho is one of my top three favorite books, and every time I read it, something new stands out. The last time I read the book, I couldn't help but feel moved when he wrote about Santiago's beginner's luck with selling crystals at the shop. The crystal shop owner says to Santiago,

> *"It's called the principle of favorability, beginner's luck. Because life wants to achieve your destiny."*

I've noticed that any time I am granted this kind of favor, I know it's something for me. It wasn't

Santiago's final destiny to sell crystals, but it was something intended for him on his journey. Whether it's something I should be doing, or just me being in the right place at the right time, I know that it's never coincidental. At the end of the book, before the Alchemist and Santiago part ways, the last thing he says to him is:

> *"Every search begins with beginner's luck. And every search ends with the victor's being severely tested."*

This means to take notice of the signs laid out for you in your personal quest. You may notice some things that will come easy for you, and that's because you're being encouraged to accept your fate. However, understand that nothing worthwhile will remain easy. There's always going to be a sacrifice and tax you have to pay on the journey to your destiny.

I've lived by this, and it has yet to fail me. Whether you call it beginner's luck, coincidence, favor or grace, it's all the same experience by the same force of power. We may not always want to walk in our purpose or feel qualified for it, but God always makes room. Not only does he make room, but when we feel lost or hopeless, you will be given some sort of sign to reassure you that you're on the right path.

Oftentimes we don't even know our purpose and

don't realize it until much later in life. We don't always find our purpose, sometimes it finds us, and it doesn't always look like we thought it would. Before I started to live in the moment, I thought my purpose was to inspire those who wanted to follow their dreams. Typical. I always knew I would have some influence in the media, and I really thought my passion for acting was the platform to help me fulfill my purpose of bringing inspiration. LOL! Of course, those things will be fulfilled, and it will be rewarding to have that experience. However, the real purpose goes so much further than that.

See the thing about trying to create and rationalize your purpose yourself, is that you involve all things earthly and don't leave enough room for God to step in and do the divine work. While I thought my purpose was just to inspire others to follow their dreams, that meant I had to accomplish mine. That meant that I had to make sure that I was the famous, accomplished, and successful person that I always thought I had to be so that I could "influence the world and inspire generations." So in my mind, to fulfill this purpose that I've created for myself, all I have to do is "whatever" it takes to be on that pedestal.

So let's just say that I still believed that was my purpose and finally received the accolades that would fulfill that purpose, then what? Does my purpose stop because I won an Oscar or a million dollars, or a mansion? Or... oh wait... do I then gain a new purpose? Does my purpose now become to be a good mother and raise good children? So when they grow up, then what? Is my purpose now to be this great philanthropist and give back to my community? So after I donate a $500,000 check to a charity then what? Do you see what I mean? In those beliefs, my purpose is ever-changing and doesn't give me the proper backbone to continue to live my life in its entirety. It's set up to compartmentalize my life in different parts as if I'm evolving to be a different person. We grow up, change every day, and learn new lessons that make us wiser beings, but our eternal spirit makes us who we truly are forever.

Our divine assignment is not attached to our physical bodies, but to our spirits. So with my past beliefs on what I thought my purpose was, I could easily either:

1. Get caught up in earthly matters.
2. Become easily discouraged because I'm being guided by earthly means.
3. Not make room for God to lead and bless my life and remain stagnant.

This is why it's important for you to really dive deep

into understanding your purpose for your life. When you try to create it yourself, you can guide yourself into something for the wrong reasons. And when your heart is not all the way in something, you won't last long in whatever it is you're doing.

After learning about my purpose and living in the moment, I now understand that my purpose is beyond the things I do, but it affects everything that I do. It is a constant no matter what I'm choosing to focus on in life, and it serves as an underlying meaning for everything I do. For example, if what you're "doing" is singing, but what you're doing it "for" is to heal, then your purpose in everything you do— beyond singing, should carry the intention to provide healing. Your friendships, family relations, people you speak with on the street, your philanthropic work, etc. should and ironically will lead to providing healing in some form.

You may not notice it, but it's there, and that's the catch-22 when walking in your purpose. You will never be able to experience the magic you bring unto others because it's coming from you. You probably won't even realize all that you are, because you're just *being* you, while other people are *experiencing* you. When you do have the opportunity to experience the magic you bring to others, it will be from

God. You experience God's love first before you can offer the experience to someone else. It all essentially comes from God; it's just channeled through you. The real power everyone yearns to have is this awareness. When you're aware of your power, that's when you are the most powerful.

HOW I FOUND MY PURPOSE

I always cherish my most intimate moments with God and the times I'm solely focused on cultivating our relationship.

These moments usually take place while I'm fasting. After I graduated from college, I fasted for ten days, and by day three, God had given me a vision of what he wanted me to do for the rest of my life. In this vision, I saw myself invested in activities I liked doing—my passions—as well as projects I would've never thought I'd be doing. I was so amazed by this vision, I immediately wrote it down and thought, "Is this really what I'm going to be doing?" Now, I didn't see a sped-up version of my life unfold before me, but God had shown me a brief vision that resonated with my heart.

Every idea given to me was designed for different stages of my life, and it almost seemed like, "Do I really have to do that?" but again, purpose is beyond you or your passions. I also find myself walking in my purpose and not even knowing it until I step back and realize, "Oh yeah… this is what I'm supposed to be doing." I also find it interesting in the timing of receiving this vision… right before I moved to Los Angeles to live out my dreams.

It wasn't until I was living in Los Angeles for a few months that God told me what my purpose was. Even after I received the vision, I was still under the belief that I was just supposed to inspire people to follow their dreams, just as I was doing. Then one day, I went to the beach to go meditate. I went to a quiet area, laid out my towel, laid down on my back, closed my eyes, and tuned in to the ocean waves. I began to fall into a deeper state of relaxation, becoming more sensitive to a higher power surrounding me.

I expected nothing more than to gain peace of mind and comfort from this presence. To my surprise, I was told what my purpose was. Clear as day, I understood that my purpose was to lead people home.

When I awoke from my meditation, I didn't fully understand what that meant. "Lead people home… so… like literally or like… symbolically? What is the symbol for home?" Then I realized it meant that I've been given the divine assignment of leading people to their source: the God that lives within them. That means getting people to understand who they are and helping them live in the space of divinity. So with this task, it doesn't mean that I have to now become an evangelist, start a church, and start preaching the word of God. No. I still get to do all the things I'm passionate about, I just now have a deeper understanding of how I'm supposed to allow my passions to facilitate my purpose. With this awareness, I can weed out all things that don't align with my purpose and are not for me. If I begin to blur that line, I will experience disappointment because my hope will get lost in things that were never mine.

Not everything for you is for your purpose, and some things that are for your purpose are not for you. As a matter of fact, it's for others. Not to say that you shouldn't utilize your purpose for yourself, but all things are for the greater good. For instance, if another actress were to receive a role I wanted, God may intend for it to be that way because it will have a different impact when she puts her hands on it and vice versa. Rather than be upset and doubt my talents, I can assess if the project was aligned with my purpose and shift my focus to walking in the open door intended for me.

We are all unique and bring our own superpower, (especially when we're tapped into it), but we're still orchestrated in a way that allows things to work for the greater good for everyone. Knowing my purpose helps me to have a better understanding of what's for me. I'm able to rely on it to help guide me to make the best decisions for my happiness and fulfillment. I know who I am, what I am, and why I am, and that is my greatest strength.

HOW TO FIND YOUR PURPOSE

Finding your purpose is something that happens in your own divine time. Whether you want to know your purpose or not, it will reveal itself to you in this lifetime. If you can't seem to figure it out, give it time, and God will let it be known to you. For starters, simply talk to God. Ask for a sign or for clarity on what is intended for you to do. After you've set your intentions to receive a sign, expect for it to come! If you set your mind on something and believe in your heart, it will come true. This is the law of attraction, God's promise… same experience, different label.

In this waiting period, be still. Continue to live life and accomplish your daily goals, but remain still in your heart and in your mind. Don't clutter them with worries, doubt, fear, or troubled thoughts. Find a way to take time to put your focus towards God in receiving your purpose. This can be done through meditation, fasting, or prayer. You can meditate for five minutes every day in whatever form works best for you. If meditating isn't for your lifestyle, you can fast. I've always done the Daniel's fast; however, you can choose your own fast. The point of fasting isn't to go on a diet where you feel like you can't eat anything. Its purpose is to help you shift your focus away from earthly things to focus on the supernatural. Much like prayer, you want to give your attention to your heart and to God because that's where the truth resides. If you do so, I promise you will gain all the clarity you need, and grace will be extended unto you.

If you don't believe in a higher power, I'm sorry because there isn't any mathematical science equation that will help you find your purpose. There is no $passion^2 + talent^2 = purpose^2$. I believe that your purpose is created from a divine and pure source, and nothing here on Earth trumps it.

PURPOSE OF LIVING IN THE MOMENT

Having a strong understanding of purpose is so important. If my "why" is not in the foreground, I quickly lose passion, become confused, and feel my actions become meaningless. I'm a person that likes to accomplish goals just to see what it feels like to be on the other side of them.

I've had several moments of getting to that other side and feeling like "…Oh… this is what it's like?" There was a time where I set a financial goal, and once I realized I would exceed it, I became filled with guilt, resentment, and fear. It wasn't the feeling I was expecting, and I hated that I felt that way. In this instance, I had to remind myself of my "why" for even setting that goal. Yes, part of it was for financial growth, but it was also to build a more trusting relationship with myself. Now, I know that if I set a goal, I am liable to meet it. I trust myself to make good judgments on what I can and can't handle. Without having this understanding of purpose, I'm sure I would still feel bad and hesitate to set and accomplish another financial goal in that same regard.

It's important to have a strong sense of purpose because you can easily get lost in the motions of life. You can get caught up in everything you accomplish, how much money you make, how much attention people give you on social media, etc., and forget why you're even in the position you are. Or even worse, you become filled with self-glorification for all the things that you do, because you thought you did all of it on your own. As we go through life, we experience every emotion, and never know what to expect. This is why it's important to learn to live in the moment. The purpose of our life lies in the purpose of living. We have to be able to experience every moment to fully understand and be a witness to God's work. The supernatural involves all things, whether you can see it or not, but it's your decision to live to see it.

It all goes back to simply choosing to be yourself and embracing all your glory. Listening to the God on the inside, and choosing pure love over ego. Rather than letting your past control you, it's about releasing your wounds and allowing every new moment to have a spotlight in your life. Highlight this very moment as you're reading this, and embrace what's now. It will never be the same, and that's the beauty of life. Ever-changing, always moving, forever-evolving, and surprising.

My journey isn't over, and living in the moment has just begun.

ABOUT THE AUTHOR

Kamri Cole is an actress and writer from Houston, Texas. After graduating from Howard University she moved to Los Angeles to pursue her love for acting. Along her journey, she discovers what it means to walk your divine path and now strives to help others walk theirs. She is the creator of the event series, ALCHEMY, a series designed to help women grow, heal, and achieve their divine potential. With ever-growing enlightenment, Kamri believes in elevating the consciousness of people and communities by connecting them through humanitarian outreach and empowerment.

CONTACT

www.kamricole.com

For speaking engagements, bookings, interviews, or book signings, please contact **kamricole@gmail.com**

○ @kamricole

f @kamricole

🐦 @kamricole_

Made in the USA
Middletown, DE
20 June 2022

67333873R00092